The STANLEY PARK Companion

Ron Bell
2003

PAUL GRANT AND LAURIE DICKSON

BLUEFIELD BOOKS

Contents

A DRIVEWAY IN STANLEY PARK

The STANLEY PARK *Companion*

Published by
Bluefield Books
Gr. 12, C. 9, R.R. 1, Winlaw, B.C., Canada V0G 2J0 250-226-7761

Distributed by
Raincoast Books
9050 Shaughnessy Street, Vancouver, B.C., Canad

National Library of Canada Cataloguing in Publi

Grant, Paul, 1948-
  The Stanley Park companion / Paul Grant, Lau

ISBN 1-894404-16-5

1. Stanley Park (Vancouver, B.C.) — History. I

FC3847.65.G72 2003   971.1'33   C2003-910
F1089.5.V22G72 2003

T1-AXA-447

Pages 1 & 144 photographs: BRENDA HEMSING
Page 3 photograph: F. GOWEN PHOTO, 1917. VA, CVA (
Page 5 photograph (opposite): PAUL GRANT & LAURII

Designed by Gillian Stead
Edited by Margaret Tessman

A Julian Ross 🦋 Bluefield book

03 04 05 06   5 4 3 2 1

Printed in Canada

Siwash Rock. CHRISTOPHER GRABOWSKI

PREFACE

A Thousand Acres

BRENDA HEMSING

I T'S A SECTION AND A HALF, ABOUT THE SIZE OF A MODEST Saskatchewan grain farm, and a shade larger than New York's Central Park. Every day its trees pump out enough oxygen for 11,700 people while providing a home for more than 200 kinds of birds and dozens of species of mammals. Stanley Park has playing fields, gardens, beaches, and hidden corners of calm retreat for the people who live in Canada's third-largest city. There's everything you need for a Sunday in the park, including an aquarium, a petting zoo, rose and rhododendron gardens, a miniature railway, a pitch-and-putt golf course, an open-air summer theatre, restaurants, and a seaside walk that circum-navigates the park and is a people-watcher's dream. Yet serenity and solitude are just a few steps away.

Take any of the leafy, inviting trails that wander off into the woods. Within minutes you're in the calm, green heart of an ancient forest. The air on your skin is noticeably cooler and your nostrils fill with the sweet tang of crushed fir needles. For a moment you can indulge in the fantasy that you're one of the few people since time began to have found this spot. You're not, of course. Eight million people a year visit Stanley Park. As many as 2,000 people an hour crowd the nine-kilometre Seawall on any given summer's day, while 70,000 vehicles cut through the middle of the park on an ill-conceived, curving, three-lane expressway called the Stanley Park Causeway. Even so, on the busiest sunny summer Sunday you can still find spots where you're utterly alone.

Stanley Park isn't just Vancouver's biggest tourist attraction. It's also Vancouver's soul, offering the elusive experience of deep and absolute calm found only in an ancient place. This green magic isn't something you buy or plug into. It's a gift from trees that could be 1,000 years old, a serenity that may be found while watching the waves pound on a rocky shore. It's the quality of stillness you introduce to your children to, hoping it will seep into their busy minds while they make friends with the bolder squirrels or scramble over the beaches looking for starfish and tiny scuttling crabs.

Unlike most large cities, Vancouver has no natural history museum, no zoological garden to inform and educate people about animals. Instead, we have Stanley Park, an oasis of flora and fauna, with species indigenous and introduced, mingling in one big outdoor laboratory just moments away from downtown Vancouver. And because the park is as old as the city, it's a historical register, too. From the middens of the Coast Salish people to the personal stories engraved on hundreds of park benches, Stanley Park is home to our heart's history. This book will tell you a little bit about all of that, and lots more besides. We hope you consider it an amiable companion on your discovery of these thousand acres called Stanley Park.

It's not as wild as it seems. This is a subtly managed, cultivated wilderness, but still primitive enough that you can sense nature anxious to regain control.

ROBIN WARD

LEONARD FRANK PHOTO, 1914. VPL 4524

1 Vancouver's Green Heart

A city that has been carved out of the forest should maintain somewhere in its boundaries evidence of what it once was, and so long as Stanley Park remains unspoiled, that testimony to the giant trees which occupied the site of Vancouver in former days will remain.

Vancouver News Herald, *1899*

IT BEGINS IN THE FOREST

THE JAW-DROPPING ASPECT OF STANLEY PARK IS THAT it's a 650-acre forest of mature trees thriving in the heart of one of Canada's most densely populated communities. And then there's another 350 acres of ornamental gardens, open fields, buildings, beaches, roads, and parking spaces. More than a thousand acres, between the city and the sea, containing nearly half a million trees, where the only constant is change.

Forests are born when enough organic matter accumulates to nourish the seedlings of the first trees that stretch upwards, past the dense shrubs and undergrowth. These deciduous trees, such as alder, leaf out each spring, and lose their leaves in the fall. As they mature and die back, their remains give other species a chance to grow, and a new forest evolves. Given enough time and the right circumstances (no fires, typhoons, or logging), trees such as the western hemlock, Sitka spruce, Douglas fir, and western red cedar commingle and establish the mature forest —a grove of coniferous and evergreen trees.

As these giants spread their boughs, the ground-level plants or understorey adapt to the deepening gloom. Salal, ferns, skunk cabbage, and bright salmonberry bushes carpet the forest floor. When a towering pine or fir tree topples, it takes down lesser trees and leaves a considerable gap for sunlight to reach the lower plants. Encouraged by the light filtering through the gaps in the canopy, the deciduous trees rise again and nurse on the fallen conifers. And so it goes — the natural evolution of a coastal forest.

Stanley Park is no pristine example of first-growth forest. It was logged three times in the nineteenth century. One account tells of a swath cleared and burned from Lost Lagoon all the way back to the north end of Pipeline Road near the Prospect Point

Note the decorative carving at the base of this big tree. R.H. TRUEMAN PHOTO, CA. 1902. VA, CVA 2-139

lookout. On October 12, 1962, the tail-end of Typhoon Frieda blew through the park, her 125 k.p.h. winds knocking down enough trees to make room for a miniature railway. So almost all of what remains is second- or third-growth forest.

There still exist hidden groves of monument trees that were too big to log a century ago. The loggers simply couldn't get high enough up the tree to find an area where they could actually cut through the trunk. These trees can be found down the Third Beach Trail near the Hollow Tree and behind the Service Road. There's also the famous National Geographic Tree, so-named because it was featured on the magazine's cover in October 1978. Tree experts reckon it's 1,200 years old. Sadly, the tree has had some drastic surgery, but you can still see its lower trunk, with a girth that's unbelievably huge.

The Stanley Park forest is now at a point in its evolution where nearly half the trees are western hemlocks. This species has never been considered "good wood" and was ignored by the loggers of the nineteenth century.

Part of a grove of close-growing trees known as the Seven Sisters. STUART THOMSON PHOTO, CA. 1912. VA, CVA 99-46

The seedlings grow quickly in deep shade and, unlike cedar and spruce which need light to establish, hemlock regenerates effortlessly in the dense understorey. The problem with hemlock is that as it grows and breaks through the forest canopy, it can become infested with the parasitic dwarf mistletoe, which rides the tree to the sky, weakening it and eventually contributing to its downfall. If this situation were left to nature, Stanley Park would evolve again into a more deciduous forest. But judicious removal of damaged trees and the spot planting of small, or umbo, seedlings (park workers call them "jumbo" seedlings) of cedar, spruce, and other conifers will maintain the forest as we know it.

These beautiful trees provide an escape into nature for local residents and a sanctuary for small mammals such as coyotes, skunks, raccoons, and the occasional deer, along with 238 species of birds. The trees also contribute to Vancouver's sparkling climate by absorbing carbon dioxide and other pollutants from the air. A healthy tree with a 75-centimetre trunk will scrub out nearly 22 kilograms of carbon dioxide each year. One acre of trees will provide enough oxygen for 18 people. No wonder those air fresheners dangling from rear-view mirrors are shaped like tiny Christmas trees.

The best way to see the trees is by walking. Step off the main road or the Seawall, onto one of more than two dozen trails, and enter the green grandeur of a cathedral forest. The vast, vaulted ceiling of branches brings immediate relief on a hot afternoon, and a quiet respite from the roar of traffic nearby. How nearby? The causeway that bisects the park funnels 70,000 cars onto the Lions Gate Bridge each day and more than 2 million cars take the scenic drive around the park perimeter each year. Obviously, the trees are working overtime dealing with all that car exhaust. Give them and yourself a break and leave your car behind. Walk, cycle, or hop the free shuttle bus and visit the trees the way nature intended.

THE STANLEY PARK SHUTTLE runs from mid-June to mid-September between 10:00 a.m. and 6:30 p.m. The shuttle stops at 14 popular attractions around the park and it runs every 15 minutes. If you do bring your car, pay parking is in effect year round. Purchase a ticket by coin or with your credit card from one of the blue dispensers.
To get to Stanley Park, take the #23, #123, #35, or the #135 bus from downtown Vancouver and you'll be dropped off behind the Pavilion, near the miniature railway.

STALKING THE BIG TREES

Early logging and slash burning and later the tail-end of Typhoon Frieda took down huge swaths of old-growth forest in Stanley Park. Still, there are a few remarkable stands of trees remaining north of the Park Drive between Prospect Point and Siwash Rock, and off Pipeline Road just north of the miniature railway. The area between Lost Lagoon and Beaver Lake was heavily logged in the nineteenth century, but some of the forest giants were too massive to cut down and bring out at that time. The really big boys are the Douglas firs, which can soar to nearly 100 metres. Unfortunately, many of the more spectacular specimens have been topped for safety reasons — the Park Board simply can't risk one of these trees toppling in a windstorm. There are some trees to look for, though, that will give you a sense of the size these forest giants can attain.

The Hollow Tree was a popular photo spot for park visitors. From left to right: unknown woman, Norman Carmichael on McVie Carmichael's lap, Marion Grace Carmichael in Nurse Weir's arms, Mrs. Elsie Carmichael (nee Conacher).
PHOTO COURTESY ANNE DUKE

The current largest living tree in the park is a Douglas fir just north of Lost Lagoon at the intersection of Lees and Cathedral Trails. Standing at the juncture, face east and look towards the left side of Cathedral Trail. The tree's diameter is only 2.5 metres but it's more than 61 metres tall, and that's after it has been topped. The bark on a Doug fir is deeply grooved, and a square notch taken out of the bark scars this particular tree. An eagle has made its home in the upper branches.

There's a taller, though only partially-living, Doug fir that can be viewed from Pipeline Road, near the road sign indicating a sharp right turn. If you look east at this point you'll find a stand of several large firs. It's in there and is estimated to be around 76 metres tall.

The Hollow Tree is perhaps the most famous tree in the park, but another western red cedar made the cover of *National Geographic* magazine in October 1978. The two trees are quite close together near the Third Beach Trail.

You don't even have to get out of your car to see the Hollow Tree. The Park Drive skirts around the tree on both sides and a picnic area is conveniently located nearby. There are more archival pictures of the Hollow Tree than of all the other attractions in Stanley Park. From the late nineteenth century, people were posing inside the tree in wagons, buggies, cars, trucks, bicycles — you name it. Now a veritable shell of its former self, the rugged old tree is tightly flanked by a pair of western hemlock that keep it braced upright. Its diameter is impressive, 5.5 metres, the largest diameter of any tree in the park, dead or alive. No one is sure how the tree died, but it was probably struck by lightning.

The park's tallest western red cedar has taken quite a battering since its cover model days of 30 years ago. The National Geographic Tree was topped, and then further truncated by a windstorm, but it's still a mighty presence at 40 metres. You'll find it on the east side of the Third Beach Trail leading down from the Park Drive near the Hollow Tree. If you're heading down from the road, it will be on the left-hand side — you can't miss it.

There are a couple of notable deciduous trees in this area as well. Just northwest of the concession at Third Beach towers the largest red alder in Canada. It's 30 metres tall with a diameter of 1.8 metres. It stands right next to the wooden viewing platform behind the concession on the bluff above the Seawall. And a bigleaf maple, believed to be the largest in Canada, is found directly south of the Hollow Tree at the spot east of Rawlings Trail and just north of the Lake Trail. It's 39 metres tall and 3.4 metres in diameter. And yes, the leaves are big!

The greatest damage to these old trees can occur when they're at their most beautiful. It rarely snows in Vancouver, but when it does Stanley Park becomes a magical place. The woods are utterly silent and the old conifers loom massively beneath the blanket of snow. Coastal snow is wet and dense and the weight of it can rip the slender branches off a tree. If there is rain before a snowfall, it just makes matters worse. In soggier, shady areas, trees have very shallow roots. A combination of snow, wind, and too much rain can easily bring down a shallow-rooted tree. Be very careful on the trails during the winter.

If you're caught up in the hunt for big trees, there have been reports of a 99-metre giant Douglas fir. Though various sources claim to have seen it, no one is revealing its exact location. Happy hunting!

Compiled from *Hiking Guide to the Big Trees of Southwestern British Columbia,* by Randy Stoltmann. Western Canada Wilderness Committee, 1987. Ground-truthed by members of the Stanley Park Ecology Society.

Heavy snow is unusual in Vancouver and can damage tender tree branches. Even the swans seem surprised.
STUART THOMSON PHOTO, 1919. VA, CVA 99-248

An eight-foot deep midden of shells left by the Squamish people who used Stanley Park as a summer camp for thousands of years. Park workers dug up the shells and crushed them to pave Park Road.   CHARLES S. BAILEY PHOTO, 1888. VA, SGN 91

2 The Stanley Park Story

To the use and enjoyment of peoples of all colours, creeds, and customs,
for all time, I name thee Stanley Park.

Lord Stanley, October 29, 1899

THE HISTORY

PEOPLE HAVE BEEN LIVING ON THE PENINSULA WE CALL Stanley Park for at least 8,000 years. The Squamish people used the area around what is now Lumberman's Arch as a summer camp. Oral histories recount great feasts, or potlatches, held at the site, where up to 2,000 people ate, danced, and exchanged gifts. Captain George Vancouver no doubt saw their large village, Khwaykhway (whoi-whoi), as he sailed past in 1792, exactly 300 years after Columbus charted eastern North America. Captain Vancouver actually thought Stanley Park was an island, as did the Spanish explorer Galiano. But then, Vancouver missed the massive mouth of the Fraser River, too.

Khwaykhway was destroyed in 1888 (coincidentally, the year Stanley Park was created) by a smallpox epidemic. The buildings were razed and the survivors were moved out. A nearby midden, or refuse heap, of calcified seashells ran beside the shoreline for about three acres, with the shells laying over two metres deep. These shells were ground and used in place of gravel to surface Park Road, which took people from the park entrance on Coal Harbour around Brockton Point and a long distance towards Prospect Point. The midden, though severely pillaged, still holds interest for anthropologists, and the sharp-eyed walker may yet find traces of materials near the clearing at Lumberman's Arch. Another midden, believed to be three times the size, was found at what is now Third Beach.

The changes to Stanley Park's primeval state began decades before the destruction of Khwaykhway. As many as five logging companies began taking timber out of the park in the 1860s. In 1865 it was suggested that the area from Brockton Point to Lumberman's Arch be turned into an industrial zone. But the currents in Burrard Inlet forced Captain Edward Stamp to locate his sawmill in False Creek instead (Stamp's Landing).

The Brockton Point area was also proposed as the site for a cemetery. In 1875 the area between Beaver Lake and Lost Lagoon was clearcut and burned. And in 1885, the Canadian Pacific Railway asked for the eastern half of the peninsula. Instead, the CPR was given a chunk of the West End and most of the Coal Harbour foreshore east of Stanley Park.

Cougar, black bear, wolves, elk, and blacktail deer were among the animals living on the peninsula in those days, along with squirrels, skunks, raccoons, coyotes, and other small mammals. Offshore, humpback whales could be seen "spouting their defiance at the millmen," according to the *Victoria Colonist* newspaper in 1869. Now, barely 60 percent of those creatures remain in or around the park. Only 25 years ago, deer were still a problem in the park, according to Mike Mackintosh, who is now the supervisor for Queen Elizabeth district parks in Vancouver, and de facto manager for wildlife services with the Vancouver Park Board.

"At one time when I first started working in Stanley Park," he recalls, "we used to have deer swimming across from the North Shore on a regular basis every summer and feasting on the Rose Garden."

In 1886, much of Vancouver was still forest and farmland. Yet the first resolution by the newly minted Vancouver city council asked the government of Canada to authorise "that the

Squamish elder August Jack Khahtsahlano was the grandson of Chief Chaht-sah-lanough, who lived in the village on the site where Stanley Park was dedicated in 1889.
RICHARD J. STEFFENS, STEFFENS-COLMER PHOTO, 1932. VA, LP 3

A family outing (ca. 1890) to Stanley Park meant hitching up the wagons and putting on the fancy hats. VA, SGN 118

whole of that part of Coal Harbour Peninsula known as the Government Reserve be conveyed to the City of Vancouver for a Public Park." It now seems quite wonderful that the first civic government had the foresight to preserve a huge chunk of forest for future generations.

Of course, a more cynical mind might think that a pragmatic reason lurked behind the motion. Most of the councillors in those days were also landholders, so perhaps it was in their best interest to keep the government reserve off the real estate market, in order to enhance the value of their own properties. Whatever the reason, it took a year for the paperwork to go through, and another 15 months before the park was officially opened on September 27, 1888. The Governor General of

*More elegant head gear on display
at the beach near Brockton Point.*

CHARLES S. BAILEY PHOTO, CA. 1889.
VA, SGN 133

Canada, Sir Frederick Arthur Stanley, dedicated the park in his own name on October 29, 1889. A decade later, the City of Vancouver paid the federal government one dollar for a renewable 99-year lease on the park. That lease has since been renewed.

People continued to live in the park long after it was created. Many of the so-called squatters had been living on the peninsula for generations but few could prove it, so in the 1920s the city, Park Board, and federal government combined forces in court to evict them. Still, some managed to stay on. The last resident of Stanley Park, Tim Cummings, kept his home in the park until his death in 1958, at the age of 77.

The park remains a sort of home to dozens of homeless people. During the last census in May 2001, teams of enumerators swept through the park at night to count the people "living rough" there. Statistics Canada estimates that a couple of hundred people were camped out at that time, including transients, mentally ill persons, and other homeless people. The numbers decrease in the winter months, to an estimated 40 or 50 stalwart souls.

At first, the only way to get from Georgia Street to Stanley Park was to cross a log anchored in the mud flats that separated Coal Harbour from what is now Lost Lagoon. Once the park was created, a bridge was built, then replaced in 1916 with a causeway. Pipes still allowed salt water from Coal Harbour to flow under the causeway into the tidal flats to the west. But in 1929 those pipes were shut off and the tidal flats were turned into a freshwater lake called Lost Lagoon.

During the 1920s and 1930s, Second and Third Beaches were built up from a wild and rocky tree-lined foreshore to something approaching the sandy playgrounds they are today. The fill used for Second Beach consisted of everything from street sweepings to sand dredged from the deepening of False Creek. In 1962, sand from the Siwash Rock area was pumped onto Third Beach, expanding the area by about two acres.

The Vancouver Park Board approved plans for the Lions Gate Bridge, at least as those plans affected Stanley Park, in November 1933. The bridge was a private project undertaken by a group of British investors who had real estate holdings on the North Shore. It was opened in November 1938, and named for the twin peaks to the northwest. The two massive concrete lions were installed at the south end of the bridge in 1939, the last pieces of public sculpture by Charles Marega, who also created the Harding Memorial in Stanley Park and other public monuments around Vancouver.

Henry Avison was the first Stanley Park ranger. Here, (ca. 1896) he tends the garden with his son outside the ranger's cottage. VA, S-5-4

During the Second World War, parts of Stanley Park were taken over by the military. Deadman's Island was transferred to the Department of National Defence in June 1942. Despite pleas from many quarters, the military refuses to leave the island, and occupies it still. From 1941-5 the Royal Canadian Artillery manned a gun emplacement and ammunition magazine at Third Beach. And you can still find evidence of the searchlights that were installed on the bluffs above Siwash Rock.

Except for the empty polar bear caves just south of the Aquarium, there's little left of the zoo that once existed at the heart of the park. But a zoo of some sort was part of the park from its inception. The park's first ranger, Henry Avison (for whom one of the trails is named), gathered an informal menagerie and built a bear pit in 1893. By the early 1960s, the zoo contained monkeys, penguins, exotic birds, otters, seals, snakes, bears, and even a sad-looking ocelot in a glass-walled enclosure barely big enough for it to turn around in. Still, for many of us growing up in Vancouver in the 1950s and 1960s, the zoo *was* Stanley Park. It was the destination for many family outings. We laughed at the monkeys' shenanigans and the seals' sloth, but our favourites were the otters, who cavorted in a pool in front of the Aquarium. No one can say those slippery devils weren't enjoying life.

There had always been critics of the zoo in Stanley Park, and by the late 1980s they had gained the upper hand. Anthropomorphic movies such as *Free Willy* fuelled the debate about humans' right to keep animals in captivity, especially highly intelligent species such as killer whales. Mike Mackintosh, manager of the zoo at the time, remembers the battle vividly.

"We had an old facility that just didn't measure up," Mackintosh explains. There were plans in the works to redevelop the zoo for native BC species, and to create conservation programs that would take advantage of Stanley Park's diverse habitats. But in 1990 the Stanley Park Task Force started the process that put an end to those plans.

The Task Force was made up of a broad range of people. For close to two years it held extensive public discussions on all aspects of the park, from the forest and fauna to the Seawall, transportation, recreation, ownership, funding, and the future of the zoo. The diversity of opinion offered concrete and exhaustive evidence of how passionately Vancouverites care about Stanley Park. In its final report in 1992, the Task Force recommended, among other things, that the zoo be phased out and returned to green space. A plebiscite to that effect passed by a margin of four percent.

It fell to Mackintosh and his crew to find homes for all the animals, a process that took years. But he takes pride in and some consolation from the fact that zoo staff managed to place all the animals, from penguins to monkeys to sea otters, in state-of-the-art, habitat-style zoos from Seattle to Chicago. The few bears that were left, including a 37-year-old polar bear named Tuk, were allowed to live out their lives at the Stanley Park zoo. The concrete foundations of the bear pits are used as settings for local movie shoots and even art installations, as well as for

Tuk the polar bear plays coy with the crowd.
Bears remained for a time as inhabitants of the Stanley Park
zoo after it was phased out starting in 1992. STUART MCCALL

shelter by homeless people.

In an effort to limit the number of cars in the park, the Task Force recommended the creation of a free Stanley Park shuttle bus park-and-ride system and the improvement of public transportation to the park. This system has been implemented, to good effect. The Task Force also suggested phasing out the pool at Second Beach, removing wheeled traffic from the Seawall (except for wheelchairs and strollers), and constructing perimeter and internal cycling paths. These recommendations have yet to be acted upon. But as it has for more than a century, Stanley Park continues to generate the sort of spirited discussion and active use that is reserved only for something that's dearly beloved.

Stanley Park is a gathering place for all kinds of people engaged in a wide variety of pursuits. Ethnic groups from Celts to Koreans hold their gatherings in the park. Sports, boating, cycling, and other events fill the park's year-round calendar.

The largest Terry Fox run in Canada takes place every September in Stanley Park. Terry Fox was from Port Coquitlam, east of Vancouver. He was just 18 years old, and active in sports, when he lost a leg to cancer in 1977. Three years later, he decided to run across Canada in what he called the Marathon of Hope, to raise money for cancer research. His unique hop-skip step endeared him to millions of Canadians as he ran a marathon a day — 46 kilometres. Fox dipped his artificial leg in the Atlantic Ocean at St. John's, Newfoundland, and covered 5,373 kilometres before he was forced to stop near Thunder Bay, Ontario, because the cancer had spread to his lungs. He died less than a year later on June 28, 1981, at the age of 22. Close to $300 million has been raised in his name since then, through Terry Fox runs across the country. Along with the Terry Fox run, Stanley Park hosts walks and runs throughout the year that benefit a myriad of charitable causes. Their success shows yet again how important the park is to Vancouverites.

Part of the Seawall, looking southeast, across Coal Harbour to downtown Vancouver.

3 Along the Seawall

His heart was always in Stanley Park. And he is too.

Park Board communications officer Terri Clark,
on Seawall master stonemason James "Jimmy" Cunningham

THE SEAWALL

IF YOU ONLY HAVE TIME TO DO ONE THING WHILE YOU'RE IN Vancouver, walk the Stanley Park Seawall, or at least a part of it. Watching the weather unfold over Burrard Inlet and the North Shore mountains is a tonic at any time of the year. The water may be blue-green and sparkling, or a dull battleship grey, but it's always bustling with boats and seaplanes coming and going under or over the Lions Gate Bridge. The Seawall has lanes separating walkers and wheelers. But there's always a certain amount of anarchy as runners, walkers, amblers, cyclists, bladers, strollers, and large families weave in and out of the human river of traffic flowing along the path. All wheeled traffic (bikes, rollerblades) must go in the same direction, counterclockwise from Georgia Street. Walkers can go either way. Up to 2,000 people an hour use the Seawall during the summer. It's the best people-watching place in the city.

Portions of the Seawall were started along English Bay, on the western side of the park, as early as 1912. But construction of the perimeter walk began in earnest in 1917, mostly to protect the foreshore from tidal erosion. The Seawall was built in sections, as money became available. In 1920, a crew of 2,300 men worked on it, and during the Depression gangs of relief workers put their muscle to breaking and hauling rocks for the wall. The greatest individual contribution to the project came from master stonemason James "Jimmy" Cunningham, who devoted 32 years of his life to it. Terri Clark of the Park Board remembers Cunningham as a great guy and a terrific manager:

"He had a wonderful personality and he was dogged," she recalls. "He would fight for money for the Seawall because it was good work and people took a lot of pride from it. Even after he retired, he would come down every day to have coffee with the guys. He was a master stonemason for so long and this project was so dear to him. His heart was always in Stanley Park. And he is too."

James Cunningham died in 1963 at the age of 85, before he could see his dream realized. It took another 17 years before the job was done. Today, the Stanley Park Seawall links up with the Seaside Bike Trail that follows the shoreline around English Bay, then west through False Creek and, with a few interruptions, out to Spanish Banks below Point Grey. In a wave-polished nook near Siwash Rock, there's a commemorative plaque for the master stonemason, and Cunningham's ashes are part of the wall.

There are other memento mori scattered throughout the Seawall. Some of the coping stones are recycled headstones from Vancouver's Mountainview Cemetery (between 31st and 41st Avenues along Fraser Street). In the 1970s, city council passed a bylaw requiring all headstones to be flat (to ease mowing around gravesites). Families were asked if they wanted the headstones of their dearly departed, but very few did. The upright granite headstones, taken mostly from the 1919 section of the cemetery, were sanded off and used to top off a portion of the Seawall, and as part of a retaining wall at the southern end of Ceperley Park. We're certain Jimmy Cunningham would approve of such thrift.

If you plan to tour the park by car, allow at least one hour to follow the Park Drive, which pretty much parallels the Seawall. An hour will provide enough time to stop off at a few points of interest. If you're cycling, give yourself a couple of hours to complete the circumference. Follow directions and make sure you're flowing with traffic. Like the Park Drive, the Seawall bike route is counter-clockwise and cyclists share a lane with rollerbladers. There are places where you'll have to walk your bike for a minute or two. Most people don't walk the entire nine-kilometre circumference of the Seawall. If you do decide to walk it all, give yourself four hours and count on making a few pit stops along the way.

There are two main entrances to the park. You can head west on Beach Avenue along English Bay. Or you can come in off Georgia Street, which leads you onto the Seawall along Coal Harbour, then counter-clockwise around the park. This is the way all traffic (except those on foot) flows through the park. It's pretty easy to follow — just keep the water to your right.

The Devonian Park is the segue that bridges downtown Vancouver and Stanley Park. This open area offers excellent views of the marina, the Rowing Club, and the Bayshore Hotel, where billionaire Howard Hughes and his entourage holed up on the top two floors for several months in 1972. Devonian Park breaks out of the concrete canyons of office towers and condominiums lining the Coal Harbour shoreline.

View of the Stanley Park Seawall as the Canadian Empress liner enters Burrard Inlet.
Construction on portions of the Seawall began in 1912 and continued for decades.
STUART THOMSON PHOTO, CA. 1920. VA, CVA 99-1476

The Seawall has always been a great boat-watching venue.
And people-watching too.   LEONARD FRANK PHOTO, CA. 1920.   VA, CVA 99-1476

Across Georgia Street on the corner of Chilco, a massive mural decorates the wall of a large and ornate building. Dana Irving painted the chocolate-box scene for the mansion's owner, Dr. Stanley Ho. The building is a private home, and many West End residents were dismayed when it went up in 1996. The Stuart Building was a Vancouver landmark, that had occupied the corner of Chilco and Georgia since 1909. It was torn down in 1982 following a lengthy battle over the building's heritage value. The developer didn't rush into construction, hoping the controversy would die down. A design by architect Ernest Collins was selected for the site — he envisioned a matching pair of buildings with aesthetic references to the Stuart Building. Neighbours still grumbled; they complained they had lost their choice view of Lost Lagoon. In a goodwill gesture, Dr. Ho commissioned the mural to replace the lost vista. The second structure hasn't been built yet, but if it is, Dr. Ho's mural, like Lost Lagoon, will be blocked from view.

The Chapel in Stanley Park, which arranges weddings for Asian tourists, operates out of the main floor of the Ho residence.

Governor General Georges Vanier unveiled the Lord Stanley monument in March 1960. CHRISTOPHER GRABOWSKI

Vancouver is still considered a safe and affordable holiday destination for tourists from China, Japan, and Korea. And a wedding in the wilds of Canada is definitely an added attraction. Stanley Park, with its many gardens, ponds, and willow-draped bridges is a natural choice for wedding photographs. The chapel has no official connection with the park except for its proximity, and Park Board communications officer Terri Clark says that as long as they follow the rules, anyone can get married in Stanley Park:

"We tell people (to have) small weddings, stand-up, no throwing of anything, no seats, in and out, you can't erect anything, first-come, first-served, and you can't cause any kind of obstruction for people in the park."

Before the Seawall begins there is a wide, stone promenade arching over the Park Drive below. Lord Stanley's statue is at the formal entrance where his open arms welcome visitors. The statue was erected to honour a promise made by Vancouver's mayor David Oppenheimer to Lord Stanley, that a commemorative monument would be erected to depict the dedication of the park. There was some controversy about who would pay for it, and where the statue would be placed, but eventually everything was settled and Governor General Georges Vanier unveiled the monument in the pouring rain on March 10, 1960.

The original ceremony to open the park was held on October 29, 1889, near the north of end of Pipeline Road. A small cairn of stones was erected on the spot. The area was seldom visited and years later, workers used the stones from the cairn to repair the road. Not a sentimental lot, the stonemasons were loath to let any good rock go to waste. Happily, the statue still stands. And Lord Stanley's words are inscribed on its granite base: "To the use and enjoyment of peoples of all colours, creeds, and customs, for all time, I name thee Stanley Park."

UP TO 2,000 PEOPLE AN HOUR USE THE SEAWALL DURING THE SUMMER.
CYCLISTS, BLADERS, JOGGERS, AND WALKERS SHARE SPACE ALONG THE NINE-KILOMETRE LOOP. STUART McCALL

THE SEAWALL OFFERS SUPERB VISTAS OF THE YACHT CLUB AND DOWNTOWN VANCOUVER.   CHRISTOPHER GRABOWSKI

COAL HARBOUR. KEVIN MILLER

THE EMPRESS OF JAPAN FIGUREHEAD *(page 55)* WAS RESTORED IN 1928
TO HONOUR THE EMPRESS LINER THAT CARRIED CARGOES OF SILK FROM JAPAN TO VANCOUVER.   CHRISTOPHER GRABOWSKI

ROWERS IN THE MORNING MIST OF COAL HARBOUR SKIRT A FLOATING GAS BARGE USED TO REFUEL MARINE TRAFFIC. ROB CARLSON

THE RED AND WHITE BROCKTON POINT LIGHTHOUSE
WAS BUILT IN 1915 TO REPLACE THE ORIGINAL MANUALLY OPERATED LIGHTHOUSE AND FOG BELL.   KEVIN MILLER

THE MAN IN THE MOON WATCHES OVER A COUPLE ENJOYING AN EVENING WALK ON THE SEAWALL.
STUART McCALL

"JEWEL OF THE PARK." LIMITED EDITION ETCHING BY BARB WOOD

VANCOUVER ROWING CLUB

The choice before you now is whether to bear right and take the lower Seawall or to follow the upper path which takes you into the artist's walk, past the statue of Robbie Burns and the Queen Victoria monument and eventually up to the Aquarium. If you choose the lower path you'll walk past the handsome wooden home of the Vancouver Rowing Club. This heritage building, designed by architect J.W. Keagey in the Tudor Revival style, was built in 1911 to serve as a banquet facility and clubhouse for a variety of sports played at Brockton Point.

Near the end of the nineteenth century everyone was mad for rowing, and an Ontario oarsman, Ned Hanlan, was world champion. The Vancouver Boating Club was incorporated in 1886, when much of Vancouver was still wilderness, to provide recreation for the young men who came west with the CPR. The list of first members reads like a Vancouver street directory: Graveley, Ferguson, Tatlow, Cambie, and Salsbury. A clipping from the *Montreal Star* newspaper in 1886 attests to the vigorous outdoor life of our early settlers: "British Columbians say it is so healthy out there they had to shoot a man in order to start a cemetery."

In 1899 the boating club joined with the Burrard Inlet Rowing Club to form the Vancouver Rowing Club. Membership was a passport into Vancouver society, and the club hosted the young city's most prominent events. The club held strictly to rowing until 1908, when it expanded into rugby as a way for members to keep fit during the off-season. In 1911, when the club moved into its present accommodations, it began adding other sports to its agenda, including yachting, cricket, tennis, hockey, and jogging.

Canada has long been a dominant force in international rowing competitions, and the Vancouver Rowing Club played an important role in that illustrious history. The club's four-oared crew brought home the silver medal from the 1924 Olympics in Paris (the games romanticized in the 1981 film *Chariots of Fire*). The Vancouver Rowing Club's greatest era began with the appointment of Frank Read to coach the club's University of British Columbia student rowers in 1949. He established a winning legacy that included one gold and two silver Olympic medals, and a gold at the 1954 British Empire Games held in Vancouver. In all, the club won seventeen international medals in Olympic, Commonwealth, and Pan American Games competitions before Canada stopped sending club teams in the 1970s. Recently, two club members came home with gold from the 2002 World Masters regatta.

A 1,500-metre rowing course runs east of the clubhouse towards the dock where the seaplanes land. Air and sea traffic is extremely heavy in Coal Harbour. Vancouver is Canada's busiest

port, and rowers often need to battle for their right of way on the water. There are no boat rentals for the public, but guest moorage is available. Prince Philip, the Duke of Edinburgh, is the Vancouver Rowing Club's royal patron and his son, Prince Andrew, is a lifetime member. It's a private club but membership rates are reasonable, about $400 a year for adults and a summer fee of under $100 for teens.

Vancouver Rowing Club, ca. 1920.
Club members have brought home Olympic,
Commonwealth, and Pan American Games medals.
STUART THOMSON PHOTO. VA, CVA 99-1482

For more information check out their Web site:
www.vancouverrowingclub.com

ROBBIE BURNS MEMORIAL

With the Rowing Club to your right, look up the grassy hill to your left and you'll see a trim bronze figure in eighteenth-century attire. Most of British Columbia was mapped and opened up by Scottish explorers, cartographers, botanists, fur traders, and merchants from the Hudson's Bay Company. A healthy contingent of their descendants still thrives on the Lower Mainland. So of course there's a statue of ploughman poet Robbie Burns, put up in 1928 by the Vancouver Burns Fellowship. The statue is one of three copies of George Lawson's 1884 original that stands in Ayr, Scotland, where Burns was born (the other two are in Detroit and Canberra). Plaques around the sides of the pedestal commemorate three Burns poems, "The Cotter's Saturday Night," "To A Mouse" (1785), and the horse and rider that depict "Tam O'Shanter" (1791).

Robbie Burns statue, ca. 1940.
JACK LINDSAY PHOTO. VA, CVA 1184-2705

QUEEN VICTORIA'S MEMORIAL

After Queen Victoria died in 1901, Vancouver school kids began collecting their pennies to put toward a memorial to the grand old monarch, who reigned over Britain for more than 60 years. Patriotic concerts and other community fundraisers added to the pot, and on May 24, 1909, Vancouver's first city-commissioned sculpture was unveiled.

James Blomfield, who also designed Vancouver's early coat of arms on the Burrard Bridge, cast Victoria's memorial in bronze. Blomfield took the Queen's likeness from a piece by Thomas Brock, the sculptor for Victoria's Jubilee coins in 1897. The bronze was cast in England, but the granite comes from Nelson Island, on the Sunshine Coast just north of Vancouver. It's one of the largest blocks of stone to ever come into the city.

Water originally flowed into two bronze cups hanging from chains. Because of vandalism the Park Board has shut the water off. If you're a pedestrian or cyclist on the lower path, shrubbery will screen this monument from view, but it's directly to your left as you drive along the road, not far from the Burn's Memorial.

SALMON STREAM PROJECT

Around the first curve the land levels off and you're walking alongside the Park Drive. Across the road is a parking lot with an information kiosk, snack bar, and public washrooms that are wheelchair accessible. The excellent Park Board map and other pamphlets are available free of charge. Near the kiosk and down at the Seawall are signs explaining the salmon-enhancement project that starts 300 metres upstream at a waterfall near the Aquarium, and discharges into Coal Harbour. Because of urban development, Vancouver has lost nearly all of its salmon spawning streams and this project is designed to restore a vital link in the salmon run.

At low tide, with the pungent, briny smell of the ocean filling your nostrils, you may catch sight of a heron stalking its dinner in the shallow water. Set into the Seawall at half-kilometre intervals are small bronze plaques indicating how far you've travelled.

ROYAL VANCOUVER YACHT CLUB

For close to a century members of the Royal Vancouver Yacht Club have been messing about in boats at their marina on the Coal Harbour side of Stanley Park. The RVYC was founded in 1903, and was first based at the foot of Bute Street, on the downtown peninsula. But three years later, with 187 members, the club needed more room. So they floated their clubhouse to the lee of Deadman's Island, where the Canadian government leased them a waterlot of just under 30 acres. That long-term lease continues today with the Vancouver Port Corporation.

Because of the heavy freighter traffic under the Lions Gate Bridge, vessels are prohibited from travelling through the First Narrows under sail. The tide through the First Narrows runs at around six knots — the speed most sailboats are capable of under power. So the RVYC expanded its facilities to Jericho Beach, on the southern side of English Bay to accommodate the club's sailing members. Most of the vessels at the Coal Harbour marina are now powerboats.

There are now about 2,000 active members in the RVYC. It costs $25,000 to join. Moorage is extra — $3.90 per foot per month in Coal Harbour — if you can get it. There's only room for about 360 vessels at Coal Harbour, including just over 200 covered slips. Many members tie up their boats at other marinas while awaiting space at Coal Harbour or Jericho.

Longevity is a trademark of members and their vessels. The *Rhinegold*, a 36-foot powerboat, has been a member of the RVYC's flotilla since it was built in 1911, for Colonel Colin Ferrie. His son, Jock, is now in his 70s, and is the club's honorary historian. He proudly points to the club's long history of public service, then adds that some of the history is a little more checkered.

"During Prohibition," he recalls, "there were mother ships out there at the 12-mile limit, and high-speed cruisers would come out and take booze from the mother ship and run it up the Columbia River, or into Bellingham, Washington. It was a very lucrative business and did an awful lot to stabilize the maritime community around Vancouver. And there were Yacht Club boats involved, particularly as mother ships."

In 1927, in an effort to beat the high cost of dying, some enterprising and thrifty RVYC members created the Eight Bells Club. The idea was to commit members' ashes to the sea. A bell, reputed to be from the *Empress of Japan*, was rung eight times at the end of the service, and the member's name was engraved on the bell.

The RVYC is a private club, and not accessible to the public.

Vancouver has always been a boat-loving city. The Royal Vancouver Yacht Club was founded in 1903 and has about 2,000 active members.
CHRISTOPHER GRABOWSKI

HARRY JEROME STATUE

Harry Jerome was once the fastest man alive. He was born in 1940 in Prince Albert, Saskatchewan, but moved to BC with his family at age 12 and began running at North Vancouver High School. He was the first man to hold both the world 100-yard and 100-metre records, running the former in 9.2 seconds, and the latter in 10 seconds flat. Jerome represented Canada at three Olympics and took the gold for the 100 metres at the 1967 Pan American Games. A member of the Canadian Sports Hall of Fame and the Order of Canada, Jerome died in 1982. Many runners and fans of the former World's Fastest Man have had their pictures taken beside his impressive statue, located on the Seawall just before the Nine O'Clock Gun.

DEADMAN'S ISLAND

This little five-acre island isn't included in Stanley Park's land mass. It's a military base, annexed by the federal government in 1942 for use by the Royal Canadian Navy. And the Armed Forces are in no hurry to give it back. Despite being an island, the navy named it HMCS (Her Majesty's Canadian Ship) *Discovery*, and even provides a listing for the "ship's phone" in the telephone listings. There is no public access to Deadman's Island.

The island's name comes from the Squamish or Coast Salish people, who called it Memloose-Siwash-il-la-hie, which was interpreted to mean "island of dead men." Nearby middens show that early peoples lived on the island, but its primary function seemed to be as a graveyard, as evidenced by the human remains found in cedar boxes in the branches of trees. The island was also used as a burial ground for victims of a smallpox epidemic in 1888. Deadman's Island was the site of a squatter's village from the turn of the twentieth century until the last person was evicted in 1912.

A second village grew up around 1924 on the western shore of the island. Eviction notices were served, but there were still a few houseboats around in the 1940s. By then the first-growth cedar and pine trees had been logged until the island was pretty much bare.

Beyond Deadman's Island, looking east across Coal Harbour, you can see several marine gas stations on the water, and beyond them, the white stylized sails of Canada Place hotel, convention centre, and cruise ship terminal.

TOTEM POLES

Imagine a tree-lined seashore at dusk, the cedars and hemlocks creating fanciful shapes above the flat shoreline. Now turn that image on end, and you get something similar to the profile of a totem pole — a tree sometimes 30 metres tall, carved with the faces of real or mythical creatures.

The poles are unique to the Indians on the Northwest coast of North America, and tell eloquent stories about their family hierarchies. From frogs and ravens to grizzlies and thunder-birds, each crest, or totem, blends into the next and illustrates a family's story. Some experts conjecture that poles are read from the bottom up. It's also unclear whether the carving of poles is an art form as ancient as the rainforest, or a post-contact reaction to the arrival of the first European settlers.

But one thing is for sure. The Stanley Park totem poles are a bona fide photo opportunity, which helps to explain the Kodak Corporation's involvement in the redevelopment of the site. The poles are the most visited spot in the park, and the most popular tourist attraction in British Columbia.

At one time there was a plan to re-create an authentic Indian village between Brockton Point and Lumberman's Arch. Starting in the early 1920s, four totem poles were brought down from northern Vancouver Island, with others following from the north

The first totem poles in Stanley Park were erected in the early 1920s.
JACK LINDSAY PHOTO, CA. 1940. VA, CVA 1184-2710

coast. The full village was never built, but the totem poles stood near Lumberman's Arch until the early 1960s, when they were moved to their current location.

By then, several of the original poles, which dated back to the 1880s, were badly weather-beaten, and were moved to museums for preservation. Between 1986 and 1992 they were replaced with replicas loaned to or commissioned by the Park Board. Take note of the unusual Skedans (sk'-DANS) Mortuary Pole in the far right of the back row. The original was replaced by a replica carved by the late Haida artist Bill Reid in 1962.

In 2001, the Kodak Corporation, the Park Board and the City of Vancouver joined forces to help build a new interpretive centre to replace a carving shed and canoe hut that had occupied the site since the early 1960s. Constructed of cedar and glass, the centre suggests an airy, west-coast ambience. The two pavilions support a floating roof and are joined by a glass-and-wood breezeway which uses tree-like laminated columns for support. Inside are wheelchair-accessible washrooms and a gift shop, Legends of the Moon, which is a great place to snag a souvenir — perhaps a kid-pleasing bargain such as a pack of rub-on tattoos in a native motif, or a carved silver spoon.

The area around the totem poles has also been re-landscaped to improve viewing and to provide a subtle barrier to visitors who may be too avid in their appreciation of the poles. Horticultural Note: The grove of gigantic, heavy-headed plants to the right of the poles is Angelica, an herb known for its sweet flavour.

If you return to the Seawall facing downtown you'll find an open grassy area overlooking Coal Harbour. Hallelujah Point was where the Salvation Army staged outdoor revival meetings. Their rousing tambourine-shaking and hymn-singing could be heard across the water.

NINE O'CLOCK GUN

You can hear its report every evening at precisely nine p.m., sometimes as far away as Mission, 67 kilometres to the east up the Fraser Valley. The nine o'clock gun has been fired since 1894, when it was first installed to help sailing ships set their chronometers. Sailors used the flash rather than the actual blast to synchronize their timepieces. Firing the gun was the responsibility of the Brockton Point lighthouse keeper. The first person to hold that job, William Jones, said he kept the sights trained on the mayor's office in City Hall. The gun measures two metres long and has a range of about a kilometre, not quite far enough for Jones' purpose. During the Second World War, the practice of firing the gun was discontinued to avoid alarming folks. UBC engineering students kidnapped and later ransomed the gun as a prank in 1969.

The original Brockton Point lighthouse, shown here ca. 1901, was built in 1890 and replaced by the present red and white version in 1915.

VA, S-5-6

BROCKTON POINT LIGHTHOUSE AND PORT OF VANCOUVER LOOKOUT

The first lighthouse was built here in 1890. The present one dates back to 1915, when the Coast Guard installed a fully automated light. This area was once proposed as the site of a sawmill, but the treacherous currents made landing logs here impossible. It was also suggested that the point would be an ideal place for a cemetery.

If you're walking along the path level with the road, notice the robust arbutus tree grasping the steep bank. A distant relative of the heath (*ericacae*) family, arbutus is exclusive to the west coast and notable for its lavish tendrils of peeling bark, which expose the smooth, red skin underneath. Photographers can get a shot of the tree silhouetted against the billowing white sails of

Canada Place to the east. Those five white sails, by the way, are made of teflon-coated fibreglass.

The Port of Vancouver has erected bronze plaques with trade information along the Lookout. This is a great place to witness the marine activity of Canada's largest port, although getting down from the cycle path to look at the plaques requires clambering over barriers erected at the top and bottom of the stairway.

The Port of Vancouver serves more than 3,000 vessels a year and does about $40 billion in business with more than 90 different countries. Japan is the port's biggest trading partner. Spend a little time here and you'll be amazed by all the different modes of transportation. There are the usual pleasure boats, tugs, and freighters. That little red and white ferry is Translink's SeaBus, churning across the inlet every 20 minutes, taking passengers back and forth between Lonsdale Quay in North Vancouver and the terminal at the base of Granville and Hastings on the Vancouver side. You're bound to see and hear the heli-jets and seaplanes roaring past, taking passengers to Victoria, Whistler, Nanaimo, or perhaps to isolated logging camps up the coast. They land just past Canada Place and are choreographed by the Harbour Control Centre, which coordinates traffic at North America's third busiest port.

Just past Brockton Point,

CHRISTOPHER GRABOWSKI

to your left as you drive along the Park Drive, is the *Chehalis* Cross. On a sunny Saturday afternoon, July 21, 1906, the steam tug *Chehalis* (shuh-HAIL-us) was chugging along west of Brockton Point, with a load of sunbathers on board. The CPR steamer *Princess Victoria* came around Brockton Point, cruising at about 15 knots. The skipper, Captain Thomas Griffin, said later the *Chehalis* was steering erratically, and he swung wide to avoid her. Inexplicably, the *Chehalis* cut right in front of the *Victoria*, and was T-boned. It sank quickly, and eight of its passengers were drowned. Captain Griffin was arrested and charged with manslaughter, and although he was later acquitted, his career was pretty much ruined. Besides the *Chehalis* monument, the tragedy left another lasting legacy — the posted speed in Burrard Inlet was lowered to 10 knots.

SPORTS AT BROCKTON OVAL

You've rounded the point and are situated between the totem poles on your left and Burrard Inlet on your right. The grassy expanse behind the poles is the venerable Brockton Oval, home to track-and-field meets, and games of cricket, baseball, grass hockey, and rugby.

A very civilized spot to spend an afternoon:
the Brockton cricket pitch. Tea, anyone?
STUART THOMSON PHOTO, 1938. VA, CVA 99-2920

Brockton Oval was Vancouver's premier sports field.
A pole-vaulter participates in a track-and-field event, ca. 1940.
JACK LINDSAY PHOTO. VA, CVA 1184-2524

Rugby action at Brockton Oval, ca. 1928.
STUART THOMSON PHOTO. VA, CVA 99-3031

In the early days, it was the city's premier sports field, and some legendary teams have competed here. Hollywood stars Errol Flynn and David Niven played cricket here, and members of the famous New Zealand All-Blacks rugby squad surely bent their elbows in the clubhouse, built in 1927.

In 1992, the Stanley Park Task Force found that Vancouver residents have good access to sports facilities around the Lower Mainland, so there was no need to develop more playing grounds within Stanley Park. Grass hockey and soccer have already moved onto fields with artificial turf, and major track meets are staged at larger venues. There is still a softball diamond behind Brockton Oval, used frequently during the summer. And of course there's the cricket pitch. Few games are as charming as the relaxed pace of a cricket match on a summer Saturday. The players and officials will be delighted to explain the game to you, but it may still be difficult to understand.

THE GIRL IN THE WETSUIT

Copenhagen has its Little Mermaid; Vancouver has the Girl in the Wetsuit. In fact, Vancouver's iconic girl of the sea was originally going to be a copy of the Little Mermaid. The idea originated in the 1960s, with the Vancouver Harbour Improvement Society. Sculptor Alek Imredy, who was born in Hungary in 1912 and immigrated to Canada in 1956, agreed to sculpt it. But the Danes wouldn't give their permission.

Imredy was actually relieved that he wouldn't have to copy a figure so closely associated with Copenhagen. Instead, he proposed to keep the idea of a human form set on a rock, but suggested a scuba diver instead. Scuba (Self-Contained Underwater Breathing Apparatus) diving was becoming popular in the 1960s. And though the form of the sculpture would certainly suggest the Little Mermaid, it would be a more contemporary, Vancouver creation, meant to represent Vancouver's dependence on the sea.

He sculpted the figure first in clay, and then employed the lost wax process to cast it in bronze. Three women modelled for the figure. Imredy's widow Peggy vehemently denies that she was one of them, but says many women have falsely claimed the role. The artist used his own hand as a pattern for the figure's left hand.

The Girl in the Wetsuit was originally going to be a copy of Copenhagen's Little Mermaid. The statue was unveiled in 1972. CHRISTOPHER GRABOWSKI

The statue was unveiled on June 10, 1972 to great public response, both positive and negative. It seems hard to believe now that such a dear little figure could cause such an uproar.

Empress of Japan FIGUREHEAD

The ornate dragon's head was restored in 1928 through a campaign by the *Vancouver Province* newspaper to honour the original *Empress of Japan*, a ship that carried cargoes of silk from Japan to Vancouver from 1891 to 1922. A fleet of these Empress ships raced across the Pacific, loaded with bales of silk bound for garment manufacturers on the eastern seaboard of North America. As soon as the ships docked in Vancouver, the silk was moved onto waiting trains, then rushed east. The fabric was such an important commodity that other trains were shunted onto sidings to let the silk trains roar through. With the development of man-made textiles, the demand for silk dried up and the last of the Pacific Empress fleet sailed in 1992.

PIPELINE ROAD

This road marks the right-of-way for Vancouver's water supply, which comes from the Capilano watershed, the geographical divider between North and West Vancouver. The Capilano River empties out into Burrard Inlet just west of the Lions Gate Bridge. The pipe was laid across Burrard Inlet in 1889 and runs through the park along the road. Lord Stanley's dedication ceremony took place near this spot. Don't even think about how easy it would be to sabotage our water supply.

STONE BRIDGE

At approximately the four kilometre marker on the Seawall you reach the point where Beaver Creek drains into Burrard Inlet. There's a stone bridge to your left and the path underneath leads down a gorgeous trail to Beaver Lake. Back on the Seawall, the Lions Gate Bridge begins to command your view. Depending on the time of year, you may also see people fishing for perch or smelts off the rocks below, or right off the Seawall itself. The water here is surprisingly clear, especially considering the amount of marine traffic.

LUMBERMAN'S ARCH

Lumberman's Arch is an ideal place for kids to blow off steam. Rarely crowded, it has a water park and a long, narrow beach nearby where crabs lurk beneath the rocks. The gently undulating water park lets kids in wheelchairs shoot the water cannon and splash their pals. When they get chilled, they can wheel into an innovative dryer that looks like a Dr. Seuss version of an airport security gate.

The beach and broad meadow have been enjoyed by people for more than 8,000 years. The Squamish people had a summer camp here, evidence of which is contained in the pile of seashells they left behind — three acres of shells over two metres deep. Anthropologists estimate it would have taken 5,000 years to amass this many shells.

AT LEFT: *This version of Lumberman's Arch stood until 1947 and was replaced in 1952. The classical columns are gone, but the tribute to the British Columbia lumber industry remains.*
NORMAN CAPLE PHOTO, CA. 1913. VA, LGN 726

The original arch, called the Bowie Arch for the man who designed it, was built in 1912 for a visit by the Governor General and his wife, the Duke and Duchess of Connaught. The arch was erected downtown on Pender Street, between Hamilton and Cambie — one of a dozen such arches lining the parade route. The Bowie Arch was dismantled and floated to the Lumberman's Arch site, where it was reassembled. It stood until 1947, when the Park Board decided it was unsafe and tore it down.

The arch was missed, so the BC Lumberman Manufacturers Association erected the present version in 1952. It somehow seems small and crude compared with the original, but it still serves to remind folks of the industry that brought BC much of its early prosperity.

There are no bicycle racks near the concession, but you can lock your bikes to the wrought iron railing around the plaza. There are several picnic tables where the ubiquitous seagulls are always scavenging. Be warned, though — if you feed them, expect them to pester you until you leave. Our suggestion would be to leave the concession fare for the birds, and pack your own picnic instead, or stop for lunch at the Pavilion. The washrooms down the hill between the concession and the water park are wheelchair-accessible.

Lions Gate Bridge under construction, July 1938. LEONARD FRANK PHOTO. VPL 9631

LIONS GATE BRIDGE

"The Lions Gate Bridge perfectly combines utility with art, which always conspires with nature. At night, in fog or in sun, this bridge never lets its setting down. It never seems to impose itself upon its surroundings. It becomes a part of them, and by so doing, helps to define them."

HUGH MacLENNAN

Author Hugh MacLennan's words capture the essential greatness of the Lions Gate Bridge: from any vantage point, it's a structure that perfectly complements its setting. Viewed from the Seawall it's an iron giant whose massive legs stand everfast. From afar, by night, the fine filigree of its superstructure traces a delicate arch from north to south, its lights a string of pearls gracing the neck of the narrows.

For anyone who's ever used the bridge on a regular basis, the reality is a bit more prosaic. The middle of three lanes switches alternately for north- or southbound traffic, depending on the time of day and vehicle volume. These days signal lights control the flow of traffic in each of the lanes. Forty years ago there were no lights, and the middle track was called the "suicide lane," named for those daredevils who risked passing cars on the never-ending curve of the causeway. Even today, the crossing can be harrowing for first-timers. The lanes are narrow and cars move along at a pretty good clip. But on a clear day the view from this steel-spun cage can divert the eyes of even the most jaded commuter.

It was deep in the Depression, in November 1933, when the Vancouver Park Board approved plans for the Lions Gate Bridge. The Park Board was involved because the road leading to the bridge cut right through the middle of Stanley Park. Only one commissioner voted against the idea, protesting that the road would slice through park trails that had existed for decades. But the BC government had already given its approval for the bridge project, and the Park Board was on side. Even so, public support was far from unanimous. Local newspapers waged a fierce campaign against the bridge and debate was vociferous, though few considered the impact on the park in their reasons not to build the bridge and causeway. The Vancouver Town Planning Commission opposed the bridge by a margin of five votes to four, calling it premature and inadequate. Oddly enough, the Commission thought the causeway was a good thing — it was a firebreak through the centre of the park and it opened up new areas for public amenities.

The original plan for the bridge itself was for a clearance of 61 metres above Burrard Inlet, six metres lower than the Golden Gate Bridge in San Francisco. Desperate to settle the matter, the developers offered to pay for a plebiscite, giving Vancouver voters the right to decide the fate of the bridge. On December 13, 1933, more than two-thirds of the voters said yes to the Lions Gate Bridge. While it may have seemed an outlandish idea when

*The Stanley Park Causeway runs through
the heart of the park, linking downtown Vancouver with
Lions Gate Bridge en route to West and North Vancouver.*
DON COLTMAN, STEFFENS-COLMER PHOTO, CA. 1941. VA, CVA 586-603.2

OPPOSITE: *The concrete lions at the south end of Lions Gate
Bridge, 1939. The bridge opened in November, 1938.*
LEONARD FRANK PHOTO. VPL 3036

it was first proposed in 1926, the bridge and the Stanley Park Causeway were an ideal solution to high unemployment in 1933.

But creating jobs wasn't the main objective. The bridge was actually a pet project of a syndicate headed by the British brewing company Guinness, which had vast real estate holdings on the North Shore. The syndicate had purchased the entire British Properties, 4,000 acres, for $75,000 (now just a modest down payment on one of the large houses in that wealthy enclave). With the Lions Gate Bridge providing easy access, property values were bound to soar. The final plans were for a bridge 473 metres long and 80 metres above the water at its highest point. Stanley Park would sacrifice 10 acres of trees for the 23-metre right-of-way that would run through the heart of the park

The thing about building a bridge is that it must support itself at each stage of construction. Every component needs to fit in and be held fast by the previous footing. When additional pieces are added, their weight must be accommodated until they, too, can bear the load. Construction on the Lions Gate Bridge began on March 31, 1937. Two caissons each weighing more than 2,000 tons were sunk in the First Narrows below Prospect Point to support the bridge's weight at the southern end. The caisson for the north pier was a concrete box weighing 8,700 tons. From these footings the bridge rose. Steel suspension cables were sunk in concrete blocks, then shot skyward 111 metres to grasp the steel superstructure. The construction grew from both sides of the Narrows to join up at the centre like an Olympian game of cat's cradle.

Open for pedestrian traffic on November 12, 1938, the bridge was ready for cars two days later, months ahead of its original schedule. The first ticket was sold to Reeve Joseph B. Leyland of West Vancouver and the mayor of Vancouver, George C. Miller, bought the second. The First Narrows Bridge Company operated the bridge until 1955 when it was sold to the province for nearly $6 million (the actual cost of building the bridge was $5,873,837.17). The British Columbia Toll Highways and Bridges Authority continued to charge cars a toll until the 1960s, which recouped all its costs, and then some.

The bridge is named for the twin peaks to the northwest. They were originally called The Twins, or Twin Sisters, but in the late 1880s Judge John Gray renamed them the Lions, comparing them to the lions in Trafalgar Square in London. In 1890 a story in the *Vancouver Daily World* newspaper called the First Narrows "The Lions," and the name caught on with the public. In reference to the mountaintop cats, two concrete lions weighing 6.5 tons each were installed in 1939 at the south end of the bridge. They are the last pieces of public sculpture created by Charles Marega, who died in March 1939. Four miniature replicas stand guard on the Park Drive bridge crossing over the causeway to Prospect Point.

In 1982 and again in 1994, UBC engineering students suspended the shell of a VW Beetle under the Lions Gate Bridge during their annual Engineering Week. Such stunts were intended "to draw attention to the masterful feats of professional engineers and to celebrate the skills of all tradespeople," according to the pranksters. The 1982 affair cost the engineers a $12,000 removal fee. The "gears" who engineered the 1994 stunt were never caught.

Other engineers performed an even more amazing feat when they replaced all 51 sections of the bridge's deck, one at a time, over the course of three years, ending in 2002. Periodic overnight closures allowed the project to continue, while leaving the bridge open to daytime commuters. The narrow lanes were widened, and the sidewalks made safer for pedestrians and cyclists. Despite the $125-million upgrade (25 times the bridge's original construction cost), the bridge is still only three lanes wide, and is congested for much of the day. Almost 70,000 vehicles pass over the bridge daily for a total of 25 million trips per year.

Understandably, the bridge has its share of detractors. But even they often begrudgingly harbour an abiding affection for it. And for those who love it, the bridge's shortcomings are a part of its charm. In his 1996 book, *Polaroids from the Dead* (Harper Collins), Douglas Coupland writes about the bridge's infuriating congestion. But he then poetically comments that it "looks to be spun from liquid sugar...one last grand gesture of beauty, of charm, and of grace, where civilization ends...and eternity begins."

All 51 sections of the deck of Lions Gate Bridge were replaced during renovations that ended in 2002. STUART McCALL

PROSPECT POINT

The cargo ship Beaton Park passing under Lions Gate Bridge at Prospect Point, ca. 1940.
JACK LINDSAY PHOTO. VA, CVA 1184-3368

As you near the base of the bridge and the metal infrastructure looms overhead, the clatter of constant traffic from the bridge deck overwhelms the scream of gulls. At the 4.5 kilometre mark on the Seawall, you pass through a wire-mesh gate that is locked when high waves, falling rock, or debris force the closure of this section of the wall. You'll certainly notice a freshening of the weather as you come onto the exposed side of the park.

Directly under the bridge is a sheer wall of black, volcanic rock. Look way up and you'll see one of the largest seabird colonies on the coast (or at least evidence of it staining the cliffs a dirty white). Sixty to seventy pairs of pelagic cormorants roost along the shelves and fissures of the rock face. Listen carefully and you may be able to hear their soft crooning above the hum of the bridge traffic. You'll certainly be able to smell them. Don't try to get a better view from above — it's dangerous and you won't see anything.

A DETOUR UP TO PROSPECT POINT

Many people turn off the Seawall near here and climb the steep path for a cup of tea or something stronger at the Prospect Point Restaurant. Prospect Point is the summit of the park at 64 metres above sea level, and it offers a breathtaking panoramic view of the North Shore. Across Burrard Inlet along the northern foreshore are docks, grain terminals, huge piles of sulphur waiting to be loaded onto ships, and further east, the span of the Second Narrows Ironworker's Memorial Bridge. Eighteen workers died on June 17, 1958 when a section of that bridge span collapsed into the inlet during construction.

At the north end of Lions Gate Bridge the Capilano Indian band has a reserve on the sandy mouth of the Capilano River, where spawning salmon return each autumn. To the left is West Vancouver, its architectural styles ranging from pastel apartments along the water to condos and mansions climbing ever-higher up the side of the mountain. Tyee Point pokes out below Cypress Mountain, and further west the red and white Point Atkinson lighthouse stands watch over the entrance to Burrard Inlet. Across the Straight of Georgia on a clear day you can see Vancouver Island's peaks, which reach up to 2,200 metres. Beyond Vancouver Island is the Pacific Ocean.

Prospect Point is a busy place. Tour buses, cars, and the free shuttle bus regularly disgorge visitors who browse through the gift shop, take photographs, admire the view, or dine at the restaurant. If you're driving make sure you take coins to pay for parking — $1 for 45 minutes, or $4 all day. In fact, it's a good idea to keep a supply of $1 and $2 coins (loonies and toonies) handy. Parking enforcement is vigilant, and in effect year-round.

A small floral garden is planted each year at Prospect Point to depict a message or special event. Beyond the garden is a staircase leading down to a series of stone terraces that were originally part of a semaphore station used to direct traffic through Burrard Inlet. Each terrace affords good sight lines for photographers, and provides a bench if you're looking for a romantic place to canoodle.

As with other heavily visited parts of the park, Prospect Point is teeming with scavengers. Gulls, crows, squirrels, and those masked marauders, raccoons, will be looking for handouts. The raccoons look adorable, but they will bite. Feeding them is illegal, and only makes them more aggressive.

The deck of the Prospect Point Café overlooks the bridge and is a pleasant spot to nurse a beer or glass of wine. An express line lets you purchase tea or cappuccino and hot or cold snacks. During the summer months you can catch the Stanley Park shuttle bus for a free ride back to the park's entrance.

RACCOONS

CHRISTOPHER GRABOWSKI

Two masked bandits scale the waist-high, chain-link fence separating the sidewalk at Prospect Point from the cliff tumbling down to the Narrows more than 60 metres below. With nimble paws the first raccoon pries the lid off a green plastic garbage can. The second racoon tugs on the leader's hind leg, trying to get a piece of the action for himself.

There's really no need for them to go to so much trouble. Why settle for garbage when people will hand-feed you popcorn and take your picture in the bargain? These raccoons are shameless hams, mugging for the camera, jostling to be front-and-centre in the frame. Raccoons are a nocturnal species, but those in Stanley Park are quite happy cavorting for the cameras during the day if it means they'll get fed. They're like cartoon characters, furry little Zorros. But raccoons can become quite aggressive. Make no mistake — they're wild creatures.

Those hand-like paws have sharp claws. Their teeth aren't designed to eat popcorn, but they're pretty good for ripping flesh. Raccoons thrive on a diet of small animals such as mice, frogs, and crayfish. They'll also eat insects, nuts, berries, and birds' eggs. This forage is their natural diet, and there's plenty around Stanley Park so please don't feed them. Raccoons that are accustomed to taking food from people become aggressive in their search for the next handout. That's why there are heavy fines for feeding wildlife in Stanley Park.

Contrary to our cartoon image of them, raccoons don't wash their food — they just soften it up with water and take out the tough bits before they eat it. They aren't all that clean, and can carry some nasty diseases, such as roundworm and rabies. In 1998, the populations of raccoons, skunks, and coyotes in and around the park were drastically reduced by an outbreak of canine distemper. Such outbreaks are common when numbers become too large for the habitat. But they've bounced back. Prodigious breeders, raccoons mate in late winter, bearing as many as eight young in April or May. The little ones are weaned by late summer, and ready to go out and start their own families the following spring. Throughout the year you can see several generations working the crowds at Prospect Point.

THE JOURNEY CONTINUES

The S.S. Beaver *was the first steamboat on the Pacific, having rounded Cape Horn in 1835. She ran aground off Prospect Point in 1888.*
CHARLES S. BAILEY PHOTO, CA. 1890. VA, LGN 500

From here on, you're on the windier, wilder, west side of the Seawall. Our weather usually rolls in off the ocean, and the sun is late reaching this portion of the walk. As a result it's blustery and a bit colder on this side. Near the automated lighthouse, cyclists, bladers, and pedestrians share the path. The lighthouse is functional — the waters are treacherous around the point and more than one boat has run aground on the rocks. The S.S. *Beaver*, a Hudson's Bay Company steamship that sank in 1888, is the most famous casualty. A cairn commemorating the *Beaver* is found near the flowerbeds on the upper lookout of Prospect Point.

A potato-shaped boulder with "Julian" scrawled on its side is to your immediate right just over the wall. This is not Julian, however. It is Sunz. One story has it that she was the wife of the warrior who was turned into Siwash Rock. Another story says Sunz was a vain woman who was turned to stone by the gods as she was bent over, washing her hair.

SIWASH ROCK

Legend has it that Siwash Rock is actually a young Indian chief who was turned to stone by four supernatural giants.
BAILEY AND NEELANDS PHOTO, CA. 1898. VA, CVA 677-116

Squamish chief Joe Capilano told this Squamish legend to Mohawk poet Pauline Johnson in the early years of the twentieth century. Our version of the story is paraphrased from Johnson's book, *Legends of Vancouver*, published in 1911:

A young chief and his wife came to Prospect Point for the birth of their child. In order to be clean and to impart purity to their baby, the couple went swimming in the ocean. Custom deemed that only when they were so clean that wild animals could not detect their scent were they fit to be parents. When the mother went ashore to give birth, her husband remained in the water. As the chief continued to swim, a canoe with four supernatural giants (the Transformers, emissaries of Tyee, the Creator) came upon him. When asked to move out of their way, the chief refused for the sake of his unborn child. The four, who were impressed by the chief's fearless commitment, transformed him into Siwash Rock to stand as a permanent example of "clean fatherhood." So that he not be separated from his wife and child, the Transformers changed them into two rocks, a larger one side-by-side with a smaller one, which are in the forested hillside above Siwash Rock.

For a brief, glorious interlude, Siwash Rock was home to Russell the mountain goat, who escaped from the Stanley Park Zoo in 1966. He leapt over the fence and vanished into the woods.

Days later he was seen peering down at passersby from Siwash Rock. He would clamber down from his rocky perch to forage around the Prospect Point parking lot and jump from the top of one car to another. Sad to say, Russell's car-stomping days came to an abrupt end when he was run over on the Park Drive.

The sunlight doesn't reach here until late in the day, around what would have been quitting time for master stonemason James Cunningham for the 32 years he worked on the Seawall. Set into the wave-polished sandstone just past Siwash Rock is a granite rectangle inscribed with a tribute to Cunningham, and his ashes are embedded in the wall.

THIRD BEACH

The rocky intertidal zone of Third Beach is one of the richest troves of marine life found in the park. If you visit during low tide you'll find green shore crabs scuttling under rocks and purple starfish clinging to boulders that seem to be growing molars. These tooth-like growths are barnacles, and they're very abrasive. Don't clamber around the rocks without protective footwear. Great strands of bull kelp litter the shoreline. Kids love nothing half so much as whipping the bulbous floats around like a lasso. This stuff is pretty amazing; it can grow as much as 14 centimetres a day. Third Beach is a favourite with families. Even during the peak summer season, it's less crowded and its water is generally the cleanest of all the city beaches. Check the tidal times in the daily newspaper on the same page as the weather forecast. Look for the reference to the tides at Point Atkinson — it's all the same body of water. The largest red alder in Canada is at the cliff's edge above the Seawall, just north of the Third Beach concession. It is 30 metres tall with a diameter of more than 1.8 metres.

When you visit the beach in the early morning or in the evening you may see people digging for shellfish. Illegal fishing and harvesting have been problems in the past and people are supposed to have a license for these activities. Stanley Park is a place where all plants and animals are protected, but the message doesn't always get through. There are hefty fines for poaching.

If you're riding the Stanley Park Shuttle, you can get off at the Teahouse Restaurant stop, then walk back to the stone stairs leading down to Third Beach. There's a steep ramp for people on wheels, but there's no cycling allowed in this busy area. If you're feeling energetic, get off the shuttle at the Siwash Rock stop. You'll amaze the driver, who will claim that nobody *ever* gets on or off at Siwash Rock. The path leads downhill through the ancient old trees along Merilees Trail to Third Beach. The deep forest scent of salal and blackberry will be slowly replaced by the salt tang as you near the bottom of the trail.

PAULINE JOHNSON

Pauline Johnson was the perfect Victorian eccentric, delivering her noble savage routine to white audiences in concert halls across Canada and in England. Garbed in full Pocahontas regalia (she created her costume from a Hudson's Bay Company dress tricked out with bits of fur, bear claws, and beaded belts), Johnson was one of the most successful poets of her day. Two of her poems, "The Legend of the Qu'Appelle" and "The Song My Paddle Sings," still appear in Canadian school texts.

Thank goodness she left more than her poetry for posterity. Although the poetry may be out of fashion, her personal story of straddling two cultures is a relevant and fascinating history of Canadian race relations. Pauline's mother was an impoverished English gentlewoman; her father was a Mohawk chief whose mother was the hereditary clan-mother of the Wolf Clan. The family lived near the Six Nations reserve in Ontario, and Pauline was carefully schooled in both traditions.

Mohawk poet Pauline Johnson performed onstage in faux-native costume, which included a bear claw bracelet.
COCHRAN STUDIO PHOTO, 1898. VPL 9249

Pauline Johnson's ashes were buried in Stanley Park and a memorial erected in her honour in 1922.
STUART THOMSON PHOTO.
VA, CVA 99-1328

Her father taught her to canoe, a skill she practiced all her life, and her mother interested her in the Romantic poets, especially Keats and Wordsworth. W.H. (Bill) New, the editor of the *Canadian Encyclopedia of Literature*, says Johnson's continuing place in literary history is assured:

"Pauline Johnson has never actually faded from Canadian literary history," he notes. "Contemporary native and Metis writers have been looking back to Pauline Johnson, and ... the degree to which (she) was a shrewd public performer. She was going to use whatever devices she needed to use in order to attract attention to the issues and causes she wanted to talk about, so that that sentimental face ... was something which was consciously put on."

Though she never learned an aboriginal language, Pauline was a lifelong champion of Canada's native people. After her performing days ended, she settled in Vancouver and spent much of her time with the Squamish band, transcribing the Indian legends told to her by Chief Joe Capilano. She never married, but clearly enjoyed an independence of body and a liberty of spirit that was unheard of for most women at that time. Paddling her canoe through the waters of Burrard Inlet and English Bay, she composed the poem that will forever link her to Stanley Park, "O! Lure of the Lost Lagoon."

Pauline Johnson died of breast cancer on March 7, 1913, three days shy of her 52nd birthday. She was widely mourned in Canada and Europe, and thousands of people lined Georgia Street to witness the passing of her funeral cortege. By her request her ashes were buried in Stanley Park. A memorial cairn designed by James McLeod Hurry was dedicated on March 26, 1922, by the Women's Canadian Club. It's a bit tricky to find.

If you're driving, take the first right turn off the Park Drive into the Teahouse parking lot. The memorial is on the corner where, if you take a sharp right, you'll head down the hill into the Third Beach parking lot. The cairn is on the northeast corner, in a shady spot behind and under some trees.

The stone cairn is a couple of metres tall and more than three metres around. On the shoulder of the rock on the left is carved "E. Pauline Johnson," and her profile is carved on the front of the rock in bas-relief. The memorial is a sort of shrine for many Vancouver poets and others, who leave flowers and various tokens at the fountain.

On one of our visits, on the stone ledge to the right of her image, two sun- or sea-bleached flat rocks anchored a black and grey eagle feather. A similar, smaller offering sat on the left rocky shoulder, and a pair of drying mums poked out from a crevasse just above the base.

More permanent ornamentation includes, on the right side at eye level, a paddle and the prow of a birchbark canoe carved into the rock. Under Johnson's profile, a fountain pours clear water into a heart-shaped rocky bowl. The fountain is the nexus of a very feminine "Y" in the rock. At the left of the fountain, another, larger pool of clear, cold water is partially covered by pine needles and fronds. Pauline Johnson's Indian name is Tekahionwake, which means White Wampum. Wampum is what the Mohawk called white and purple Atlantic shells strung together or woven into belts, often used as currency.

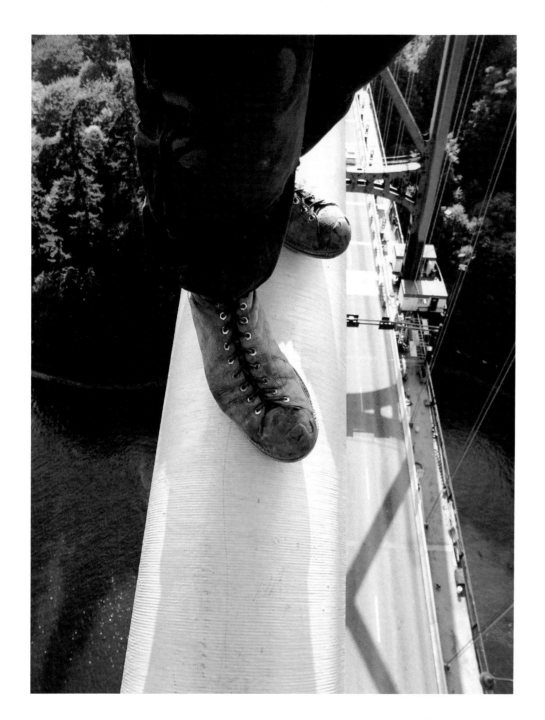

A LIONS GATE BRIDGE WORKER
BALANCES ON A GIRDER
IN A BREATHTAKING DISPLAY
OF BRIDGE BALLET FOOTWORK.
STUART McCALL

AN OPEN-AIR ART GALLERY. CHRISTOPHER GRABOWSKI

STANLEY PARK ATTRACTS EIGHT MILLION VISITORS A YEAR. CHRISTOPHER GRABOWSKI

A LICHEN-COVERED FOOTBRIDGE NEAR LOST LAGOON EVOKES THE FEELING OF A MONET LANDSCAPE. STUART McCALL

IN EARLY SPRING THE FIRST TREES TO FLOWER IN THE PARK ARE THE JAPANESE CHERRIES. STUART McCALL

THE TOTEM POLES ARE THE MOST VISITED ATTRACTION IN STANLEY PARK AND THE MOST POPULAR TOURIST SPOT IN ALL OF BRITISH COLUMBIA.
KEVIN MILLER

FALL FOLIAGE SURROUNDS
A COLOURFUL TOTEM POLE.
STUART McCALL

LIONS GATE BRIDGE.

STUART McCALL

FERGUSON POINT TEAHOUSE

On the bluff above the Seawall near Third Beach, a wood and stucco building commands one of the best views of English Bay. Third Beach was occupied by the Canadian Armed Forces during the Second World War, and used as an observation post and training camp. The Teahouse is where the officers were quartered, though the building has changed greatly from its military days. Now, it's one of Vancouver's most romantic restaurants. The floor-to-ceiling windows along the west wall give diners a full-spectrum sunset. (For lunch, brunch or dinner, the food is impeccable. But name aside, there is no afternoon tea service. Pity.) The Park Drive skirts around the rear of the restaurant and there's plenty of parking.

INUKSUIT

Between Third Beach and Second Beach, right around the 7.5 kilometre marker, you'll see dozens of little rock sculptures teetering on the boulders along the beach. Such sculptures are called Inuksuit (the plural of Inuksuk). According to Inuit traditions, an Inuksuk is a landmark used to help visitors get their bearings. They can also be used as decoys, scarecrows, or to mark sacred places. The inspiration for these little ones is likely Alvin Kanak's huge Inuksuk on the point between English Bay and Sunset Beach, just east of Stanley Park. Kanak created the Inuksuk for the Northwest Territories pavilion at Expo '86 in Vancouver. It was later relocated to its present resting spot. You can frequently find people at work along the Seawall hefting rocks in near-impossible feats of form and balance. It's a challenge that grows into an obsession if left unchecked.

SHIPS AT SEA

This is a busy stretch of the Seawall, and the path narrows drastically in some places. If you're cycling or rollerblading, you may have to slow down, or walk your bike in some spots. It's an ideal place to watch the ships bobbing at anchor on English Bay, and to figure out what they all do for a living. The crafts come in every shape and size, from tiny sailboats to sea-going yachts, and from oil tankers to cruise ships.

The most common of the working ships are the **bulk carriers**. They have cranes on deck, to load and unload lumber and other commodities. Most of the bulkers at anchor in Vancouver are waiting to load grain brought in by rail from the Prairies. The bulkers with the high, straight decklines are **woodchip carriers**. The relatively low weight of wood chips results in these vessels riding fairly high in the water, even when loaded.

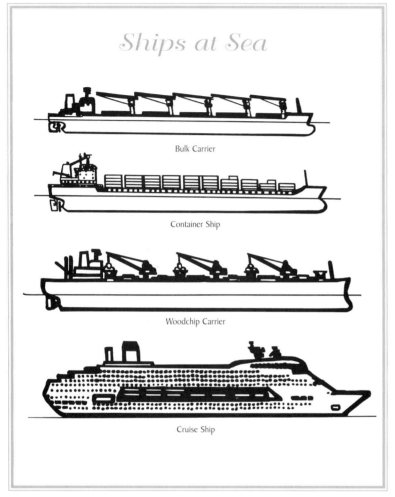

Ships at Sea

Bulk Carrier

Container Ship

Woodchip Carrier

Cruise Ship

COURTESY EILEEN MOSCA

Container ships carry goods in big metal boxes, or containers, which are stacked on deck by onshore cranes, and can be off-loaded directly onto tractor-trailer trucks. Container ships bring anything from auto parts and electronics to toys and clothing into the Port of Vancouver. Once they've been emptied, the ships load up with containers full of grain, pulp, paper, or other manufactured goods, usually bound for Asia. While the top speed for bulk carriers is about 14 knots, container ships clip along at up to 25 knots, an acknowledgement of their more valuable cargo.

Tankers are easily identified by the vertical pipes on the decks that vent gases from liquids such as petroleum products or chemicals. Some tankers have as many as three dozen separate tanks, so that if one is punctured, the leak is limited to just the contents of that tank, a safeguard that can reduce potential damage to the environment.

Finally there are the **cruise ships** — sleek, sea-going high-rises that travel between the continental United States and Alaska. More than one million cruise ship passengers visit Vancouver every year on ships with up to 2,100 double-occupancy rooms. Actually, only about half-a-million passengers call in at Vancouver, but they're counted twice — once when they embark, and again when they disembark. The cruise ships dock at the terminal at Canada Place on the Burrard Inlet side of the downtown peninsula, or at Ballantine Pier, further east on the Burrard Inlet waterfront. The cruise ship season runs from May to mid-October.

SECOND BEACH

Toddlers and penguins near Second Beach, 1952.
VPL 81894E

At Second Beach, the freshwater pool is only open during the summer months, although some hardy souls swim in the ocean year-round. This is where the cycling and walking paths diverge. The cycling path goes inland a short way, around the soccer field. From here you can turn left toward Lost Lagoon and the Georgia Street entrance to the park. Or you can explore the Ted and Mary Greig Rhododendron Garden that surrounds the pitch-and-putt golf course. To continue along the cycling path towards English Bay, bear right up the little hill past the Ceperley picnic area. There's always something going on in Ceperley Park, from folk dancing and soccer games to traffic school for tiny tots.

Walkers can follow the Seawall along the shoreline. Across English Bay, kites fly from the green sweep of Vanier Park's huge lawn, in front of the white, cone-shaped roof of the H.R. MacMillan Space Centre and Vancouver Museum. From east to west are Kitsilano, Jericho, and Locarno beaches. At the western tip of the peninsula, above Spanish Banks, is the University of British Columbia.

On the north side of the cycle path just opposite the Park Board offices at 2099 Beach Avenue is the bust of Vancouver's second mayor, David Oppenheimer. Originally from Bavaria, Oppenheimer came to Canada with his three brothers at the start of the Cariboo gold rush in the late 1850s. The Oppenheimer boys saw a need and filled it when they opened Vancouver's first wholesale provisioning warehouse, which supplied thousands of prospectors with groceries and other necessities.

David went on to serve as mayor of the young city of Vancouver from 1888 to 1891. In that short period of time, he helped to establish a transportation system that included the city's first streetcars and paved streets. He also oversaw the development of Vancouver's first civic water supply, first schools, the building of the first Cambie and Granville Street bridges (they have since been replaced), and the creation of the Park Board. Oppenheimer not only served as mayor without pay, but he donated land for parks and schools. He was instrumental in encouraging the CPR to locate its western terminus at Vancouver instead of further east at Port Moody. And it was Oppenheimer

who promised Lord Stanley in 1889 that a memorial would be built in his honour (it was more than half a century until his promise was fulfilled). Oppenheimer died in 1897 after returning to New York, where he is buried. Sculptor Charles Marega designed the Oppenheimer bust.

On the left, across Beach Avenue as you approach English Bay, is the eight-storey Sylvia Hotel, covered on two sides by Virginia creeper. Designed by Seattle architect W.P. White for Abraham Goldstein, the 77-room hotel opened on May 3, 1913, when the West End was still a neighbourhood of genteel homes surrounded by generous porches and tall leafy trees. The hotel was named for Goldstein's daughter, who died in 2002 at the age of 102. The Sylvia has welcomed any number of movie stars, writers, and entertainers, as well as several long-term residents who love its well-worn charm. In 1954, Vancouver's first cocktail lounge was established in the hotel, and it's still a swell place to watch the sun set. The Sylvia was the tallest building in the West End until 1958, when the current crop of high-rise apartment buildings began sprouting up. In 1975, the Sylvia was designated a heritage building.

JOE FORTES AND ENGLISH BAY

The name English Bay commemorates the meeting of British Captain George Vancouver and Spanish Captains Cayetano Valdes y Flores and Dionisio Alcala Galiano in 1792. That meeting also resulted in the naming of Spanish Banks, across English Bay on Point Grey.

Perhaps the most beloved man who ever splashed in the waters of English Bay was Joe Fortes (FORT-us). Seraphim "Joe" Fortes was a big man, originally from Barbados. He was a competitive swimmer and had a medal to prove it, presented by the daughter of the Lord Mayor of London. Joe arrived in Vancouver late in the summer of 1885, an able-bodied seaman aboard a disabled, three-masted barque called the *Robert Kerr*, which limped into Burrard Inlet on its way to Victoria. It was declared unseaworthy, and Joe was stranded. He worked awhile as a bartender and a porter, and eventually settled in a little cottage on English Bay, a few blocks east of where Oppenheimer's bust now stands.

Because of his proximity, Joe Fortes became de facto lifeguard at English Bay. Whenever Joe was on the beach, he was surrounded by a group of clamouring kids. He taught hundreds of them how to swim, and his reliable presence on English Bay helped to establish it as the city's most popular bathing beach.

Lifeguard Joe Fortes, the most beloved man who ever splashed in the waters of English Bay, ca. 1905.
STUART THOMSON PHOTO. VA, CVA 677-440

From Ethel Wilson's: *"Down at English Bay"*

Joe had a nice round brown face and a beautiful brown body and arms and legs as he waded majestically in the waves of English Bay amongst all the little white lawyers and doctors and trained nurses and seamstresses who jumped up and down and splashed round him. "Joe," they called, and "Look at me, Joe! Is this the way?" and they splashed and swallowed and Joe supported them under their chins and by their behinds and said in his rich slow fruity voice, "Kick out, naow! Thassaway. Kick right out!"

Joe Fortes shows off his diving style, ca. 1906. Fortes taught many Vancouver youngsters how to swim.   PHILIP T. TIMMS PHOTO. VA, CVA 677-591

Everyone describes him as a warm, friendly man. He's credited with saving 29 people from drowning during his years at English Bay, though the number could be much higher.

"Joe belonged to the beach and the beach to Joe," wrote Alan Morley in his 1961 book, *Vancouver: From Milltown to Metropolis*. "From dawn to dark and long after dark, he was host to picknickers, chaperone to courting couples, and a terror to hoodlums."

In 1910, the City of Vancouver honoured Joe with an "illuminated address," which he proudly hung on the wall of his cabin. Joe died of pneumonia on February 4, 1922. The city held a public funeral attended by hundreds of his friends and admirers. A fountain (another creation of sculptor Charles Marega) was erected near the site of his home, from funds donated mostly by Vancouver children. The fountain stands in Alexandra Park, on Beach Avenue, and depicts Joe's friendly face above three children splashing in the waters of English Bay. The inscription reads: "Little Children Loved Him." As did everyone.

Those who swam with Joe Fortes are getting thin on the ground. The little boys and girls clad in cumbersome bathing suits are now grandpas and grannies whose swimming days are mostly behind them. But the Joe Fortes legend has been amusingly preserved by the Vancouver writer, Ethel Wilson, in her short story, "Down at English Bay." *Excerpted on page 85.*

In Joe's day, you reached the beach by following trails through the bush between Beach Avenue and the shore. Once there, ladies swam on one side of a large rock, while men bathed on the other. A wooden bathhouse was built in the early 1900s, followed by a pier and a dance hall called the Prom. The current bathhouse was built in 1931, and seven years later the dance hall and the pier were torn down.

History doesn't record whether Joe Fortes participated in the first Polar Bear Swim in English Bay on New Year's Day, 1920. But about a dozen brave swimmers followed Peter Pantages into the water. Pantages was a Greek restaurateur, founder of the Polar Bear Club, and its president for more than 50 years. He urged his swimming club members to greet the new year by acting like polar bears and diving into the ocean, where the January 1 temperature averages five degrees Celsius. Some claim it's the ideal cure for a hangover; others are still feeling no pain when they take the plunge. Many polar bear swimmers make the event an opportunity to raise money for charity. The swim attracts more than 2,000 swimmers every year, while thousands more watch from the shore or from boats anchored nearby. Polar bear swims are held in many places around the world, but Vancouver's is the oldest and still one of the largest.

CYCLING

If you're cycling around the Seawall, there's really only one direction you can go: counter-clockwise. There are also dirt and gravel trails that traverse the park. Cycle with care on these paths — watch for walkers, and respect the No Cycling signs posted on some trails.

The Seawall is divided into lanes for walkers, roller-bladers, and cyclists. Sometimes bladers and cyclists share the same lane; sometimes not. Stanley Park cyclists (and bladers) range from wobblers to racers so be patient. The speed limit is 15 k.p.h., but if the path is crowded, progress slows to a walking pace. If you want to go fast, the Seawall might not be for you. Use the Park Drive instead, which also goes counter-clockwise around the park. The speed limit there is 30 k.p.h. (save some energy for the hill up to Prospect Point). Don't forget to check out the park map. Dozens of trails criss-cross the park, and these make great shortcuts and alternatives to the Seawall.

OPPOSITE: *A cycling party, ca. 1890.*
The women's long skirts and straw hats are decorative,
but must have made biking rather cumbersome.
BAILEY BROTHERS PHOTO. VA, CVA 677-277

No matter where you bike in Stanley Park, you have to pay attention. Squirrels or little kids can dart across the Seawall path right in front of you. Large families may suddenly decide to stop and chat in the bike lane. On the interior trails, watch out for wipeouts on the dirt and gravel trails. Even mountain bikes can lose their footing in the loose material. Some trails are marked No Cycling because they are environmentally sensitive. They may cross salmon streams, so try not to dislodge anything into the stream. Go gently. Take water.

Whether your bike is rented or your own, there's a chance you may have to push it back to where you started. Even bikes that are well maintained break down. Chains come off, cables snap, and tires go flat. Watch for diamonds of broken glass on the road; a sure sign car thieves have been working the area — another reason to leave your car at home. As we've mentioned elsewhere in this book, nothing is very far away in Stanley Park. So even if you're stranded with a flat tire, don't despair. No matter where you are in the park, you're not much more than half an hour from the entrance.

The Stanley Park Seawall links with the Seaside Bike Trail that follows the shoreline around English Bay, False Creek, and with a few detours onto busy Point Grey Road, all the way out to Spanish Banks, Point Grey, and the University of British Columbia.

Go fish! Playing cards in the middle of a logging road, ca. 1890. VA, SGN 139

Sunday in the Park

There's a picturesque, amateurish charm here —
all gables and rustic disorder.

Robin Ward, commenting on the architecture of Stanley Park

LORD STANLEY, I PRESUME

THE MAN WHO GAVE HIS NAME TO VANCOUVER'S LARGEST park and to the top prize in professional ice hockey in North America was neither sporting nor an outdoorsman. The sixteenth Earl of Derby, Sir Frederick Arthur Stanley (1841-1908) was shy and uneasy on the public stage. Despite these social handicaps, he was a good administrator. Lord Stanley represented the Queen with tact, a quiet charm, and common sense as Canada's Governor General for five years, before being called back to England to assume the earldom when his brother died.

Stanley Park might well have been called Smith Park. The Vancouver city fathers at first planned to name it in honour of Sir Donald Smith, one of the directors of the Canadian Pacific Railway, which owned a lot of real estate in the city. But Smith gallantly suggested it be named in honour of Stanley, who arrived in Vancouver to dedicate the park on October 29, 1889.

Virtue may be its own reward, but Smith, the first Baron of Strathcona, eventually got his park in 1911. Strathcona Park is 2,100 square kilometres of lakes and wilderness on Vancouver Island.

The dedication ceremony for Stanley Park took place just off Pipeline Road east of Prospect Point. The area was, at the time, the best grassy glade in the park and the site of a Squamish village where Chief Chaht-sah-lanough (Kitsilano) lived. There's no marker. The small cairn of stones put up to signify the event was later used by workers to repair the road. In 1960 a statue of Lord Stanley was erected at the head of the Causeway. On the plinth is carved his pledge: "To the use and enjoyment of peoples of all colours, creeds and customs, for all time, I name thee Stanley Park."

MINIATURE RAILWAY

A ride on the Stanley Park miniature railway is a rite of passage for many Vancouver youngsters. The 12-minute trip takes riders through a compound that used to be home to Arctic wolves, beavers, and most improbably, a flock of pink flamingos. The animals are now gone, though you may spot a peacock or a swan, but the little train still chugs through the big trees.

The train exists because of Typhoon Frieda. On the night of October 12, 1962 it ripped through the park with winds of 125 k.p.h. It was one of the worst storms to ever hit this area. A typhoon, by the way, is much the same as a hurricane — a violent windstorm exceeding 117 k.p.h. Hurricanes are born in the south Atlantic, while typhoons are spawned in the Pacific. The word typhoon comes from the Chinese tai fung, or big wind.

Frieda wiped out thousands of trees, and it took workers a year to get them all out. The Park Board eventually sold the timber rights as a way of removing the fallen trees. One of the hardest hit areas was where the miniature train now runs. The area was totally flattened and park planners wondered what they could do to patch up the mess.

Park Board commissioner George Wainborn came up with the idea to use the area for a miniature railway. He'd seen an ad offering for sale a miniature replica of CPR engine 374. The original pulled the first train across Canada in 1887, and can now be seen in its restored glory in the Roundhouse Community Centre on Pacific Boulevard in Vancouver. Wainborn flew to Ottawa, where the miniature train sat rusting in a farmyard. He raised the money to buy it, helped organize a group of volunteers to restore it, and 18 months later the little train began chugging out of Stanley Park Junction.

In October, the miniature railway turns into the Hallowe'en Ghost Train, taking passengers into some very scary scenarios in the fog-shrouded woods. Actors portray wicked ghouls, enchanted maidens, and other spirits, haunting the train ride every night for about a month. The family rate is around $4 per person, and includes admission to the Variety Kids' Farmyard. On weekends, in concert with the Ghost Train, the Stanley Park Ecology Society puts on an event called Creatures of the Night — spooky walks to search for bats, owls, and other nocturnal denizens. The train goes through another transformation for five weeks at the end of the year, becoming the Christmas Train. It takes passengers through a fairyland of lights, again with actors flitting through the woods, this time as Christmas spirits. Both events are hugely popular, and it's a good idea to buy your tickets ahead of time.

Call (604) 257-8531

THE AQUARIUM

If we have one piece of advice, it would be to go to the Aquarium early in the day. We arrived at 10:30 on a sunny Monday in August and stood in line for about 10 minutes. By 11 a.m. the lineup snaked out the door and down the concourse by Bill Reid's bronze whale sculpture, *Lord of the Under Sea*. The Vancouver Aquarium commissioned the work in 1984.

While you're waiting in line to get into the Aquarium, we'll tell you a little more about Bill Reid. He is perhaps the best known of the Haida artists. More than 10,000 Haida lived on Haida Gwaii (also known as the Queen Charlotte Islands) in the nineteenth century. Disease and colonization decimated and scattered the Haida. Like many indigenous people, the Haida are rediscovering their language and culture, and their art has always been strong. One of Reid's best known works is *Spirit of Haida Gwaii*, a bronze sculpture depicting a Haida canoe filled with Bear, Raven, Eagle, Frog, Man, and other creatures, which was commissioned in 1990 for the Canadian Embassy in Washington, D.C. A jade-coloured replica of this monumental work is located in the international terminal at the Vancouver International Airport.

Bill Reid's sculpture of a killer whale, Lord of the Under Sea, graces the front entrance of the Vancouver Aquarium.
VANCOUVER AQUARIUM / MARGARET BUTSCHLER

More than 60,000 creatures live in the Aquarium. There is a good representation of our local marine species as well as exotic examples of frogs, stingrays, cockroaches, sharks, and jellyfish. Tropical coral reefs have been reconstructed in floor-to-ceiling tanks visible from three sides. The steamy Amazon Gallery is alive with exotic butterflies, some the size of a robin, in all the colour combinations imaginable. They dip and flutter among the visitors, sometimes alighting on hands or heads. Outside, four different pools hold a beluga whale (a baby beluga was born in 2002), sea lions and otters, a dolphin, salmon, and trout.

The Aquarium can quickly become crowded, especially during Vancouver's rainy season when people look for indoor activities. Tour groups, large families, and sheer volume can make the going slow. You can while away a day here and not see everything. Plan to spend a couple of hours at least.

The Vancouver Aquarium is the premier educational facility on marine mammals in Canada, and perhaps North America. The Vancouver Aquarium Association was formed in 1950, and Canada's first public aquarium was opened in June 1956, in its present location in Stanley Park. It was the first facility to have scientists and naturalists mingle with visitors in the galleries, helping them to understand the interpretive graphics. It's the largest aquarium in Canada, and one of the five largest in North America.

The Aquarium does a lot more work than can be seen during a quick tour. Along with the North Pacific Universities Marine

Sea otters are voted the Aquarium's cutest residents.
VANCOUVER AQUARIUM / BOB HERGER

Mammal Research Consortium, the Aquarium's Marine Science Centre is involved in long-term research on relationships between fisheries and marine mammals in the north Pacific Ocean and eastern Bering Sea. The Marine Science Centre Marine Mammal Rescue and Rehabilitation Program provides housing and care for ill, injured, or abandoned marine mammals, and rehabilitates them for release back into their natural habitat.

In 2002, staff from the Vancouver Aquarium joined forces with U.S. officials to free a male killer whale trapped in shallow water off the coast of Washington state. The rescue attempt took weeks, and was ultimately successful not only in freeing the whale, but also in reuniting it with its pod off the coast of BC. The success of the rescue was due largely to the expertise of Vancouver Aquarium staff in dealing with orcas in the wild.

Even though the Aquarium is a world leader in orca research, there are no longer any killer whales there. Public pressure resulted in the captive whales being relocated to other aquatic facilities. But over the past quarter of a century,

Aquarium staff have been pre-eminent in cetacean research, tracking wild pods of whales on the coast and studying their social structures, their movements, and their eerie underwater language.

Our local marine life is the focus of research for the Fish and Invertebrate Research Department of the Marine Science Centre, where scientists are studying the early life stages of fish and invertebrates. They hope to raise public awareness about these creatures, and promote conservation. Our Pacific salmon is vastly important not only as a food source, but as a cultural icon. The Pacific Ocean Salmon Tracking program (POST) monitors salmon stocks as part of the Census of Marine Life project of the Canadian Department of Fisheries and Oceans. Their goal is to learn about the survival rates of salmon in the ocean, as well as habitat use and fish movement.

You can find out more about life behind the scenes at the Aquarium through Trainer Tours and Animal Encounters. Interact with harbour seals, Steller sea lions, or sea otters, while learning about the Aquarium's research and conservation programs.

Steller sea lion. VANCOUVER AQUARIUM / HANS SIPMA

WHEN YOU GO   The Aquarium is operated by a non-profit association under lease from the Vancouver Park Board. Admission is about $15 per person. There are no bike racks in the immediate area of the Aquarium. The building is wheelchair accessible, with a smooth floor. There are no automatic doors, though, and some of the doors are heavy glass. Signage is OK, but often difficult for a person in a wheelchair to see. Stroller gridlock occurs from time to time. The Clamshell Gift Shop is accessible, but crowded. There are accessible washrooms. **Web site www.vanaqua.org**

MALKIN BOWL

Marion Malkin was the queen bee of Vancouver society in the early half of the twentieth century. An ardent supporter of theatre, music, and the arts, she used her influence as the wife of one of Vancouver's wealthiest men (and mayor from 1929-32), W.H. Malkin, to bring culture to the new city. The Malkin family fortune was made purveying produce and groceries, and Malkin jam is still a staple in kitchens across western Canada. When Marion died suddenly in November 1933, her husband donated money for the construction of a performing arts space in Stanley Park. The Marion Malkin Memorial Bowl was a shell-style bandstand that replaced a gazebo similar to the one in Alexandra Park, across Beach Avenue from English Bay.

Despite the disadvantage of being an outdoor theatre in a damp climate, Malkin Bowl frequently drew large crowds, especially when Dal Richards performed with his orchestra. In 1940, someone had the bright idea of staging musical theatre in Stanley Park and Theatre under the Stars was born. In its first incarnation, TUTS was a stepping stone in the careers of baritone Robert Goulet and bass Don Garrard. The original company disbanded in 1963, but by 1970 TUTS had regrouped. The company currently stages two musicals each summer, which run on alternate nights. Cast members are local, and audiences can catch the performances of a star on the rise (Brent Carver and Jeff Hyslop performed at TUTS), as well as endearing efforts by Vancouver high-school students. Local jazz singer Laura Crema, who performed as one of the Sharks' girlfriends in *West Side Story*, recalls the rivalry between the casts of the two shows: "You always want your show to pull the bigger audience."

There have been renovations over the years, and a fire in 1983 destroyed nearly half of Malkin Bowl. It was repaired, but now TUTS and the Park Board have undertaken a complete redevelopment of the facility, which should be completed by the summer of 2005. The new theatre will hold an understage dressing room, orchestra space, a costume area, administrative offices, and public washrooms. Audiences, however, will still be left under the open sky and this fact, more than anything, determines the success of a Malkin Bowl event. Local promoters have brought in performers such as Great Big Sea, Alpha Yaya Diallo, and Joan Baez. Results have been mixed. The bowl can seat 1,500, and when the skies are clear it's filled to capacity. When it rains, well, there will always be a few stalwart fans show up. Experienced TUTS fans will pack a thermos along with blankets and umbrellas, and give their hearts over to the kids on the stage.

THEATRE UNDER THE STARS runs from mid-July to mid-August. Call (604) 257-0366 for tickets.

HARDING MEMORIAL SCULPTURE

Canada is like a good neighbour,
from whom one could borrow an egg.
PRESIDENT HARDING

An egg wouldn't have satisfied the enormous appetite of Warren Gamaliel Harding, the 29th president of the United States, who visited Canada on July 26, 1923, on his way back from Alaska during his much-vaunted "Voyage of Understanding." A week later, in San Francisco, he was dead of a heart attack, apparently brought on by shellfish poisoning. Perhaps he should have stuck with eggs.

Harding was the first sitting president to visit Vancouver. The second was Bill Clinton, the 42nd president, 70 years later. The Park Board's Terri Clark recalls that 1993 visit very well:

> For Bill to take his little jog in Stanley Park, the whole park had to be absolutely cleared from about 10 p.m. the night before. These advance guys went through the more accessible areas with a fine-tooth comb, bringing out all these people who hadn't seen the light of day in years. We found guys living in the woods, people we didn't know anything about. And then Bill's there for about 15 minutes and he had these tights on. They were kind of whitey-blue and they were some sort of weird, bullet-deflecting material.

But back to Harding. He was a charter member of the Kiwanis Club in Marion, Ohio. When he died so shortly after visiting Vancouver, the local Kiwanis Club felt impelled to erect

United States President Warren G. Harding speaking at Stanley Park in 1923. The next U.S. president to visit Vancouver was Bill Clinton in 1993. W. J. MOORE PHOTO. VA, SGN 943.17

a memorial to him near Malkin Bowl. Vancouver sculptor Charles Marega, who created several public monuments in Vancouver including the lions on the south end of the Lions Gate Bridge, was chosen to design the monument.

Part of the inscription on the Harding memorial is a quote from his speech to the assembled dignitaries that July day in 1923: "No huge battleships patrol our dividing waters, no stealthy spies lurk in our tranquil border hamlets. Only a scrap of paper ... safeguards lives and properties ... and only humble mile-posts mark the inviolable boundary line through thousands of miles of farm and forest."

There was some grumbling about this statue honouring an American president. But the complaints were ignored, and the monument was dedicated September 16, 1925, and rededicated in 1940. In 1969, perhaps in protest against the U.S.-led war in Vietnam, vandals cut the hands off one of the women, and the beak off one of the eagles. The hands and the beak have since been replaced.

Harding's administration was corrupt, scandal-ridden, and mercifully short. Little has been written about Harding, and most American histories pay scant attention to his tenure, but a recent novel, the engaging *Carter Beats the Devil* by Glen David Gold, portrays him as a sympathetic, albeit simple, character.

THE PAVILION

The chalet-style Pavilion would look right at home in one of our national parks, such as Banff or Jasper. Designed by Otto Moberg, it was built in 1911, at a time when the CPR was opening up the Canadian wilderness to European travellers. Constructed from fieldstone and wood, the lodge faces a garden and Malkin Bowl. The upper floor is used by the Stanley Park Ecology Society, which also operates the Nature House at Lost Lagoon. Downstairs you'll find a restaurant and café, both run by the Dubrulle International Culinary and Hotel Institute of Canada. Local artist and heritage expert, Robin Ward, offered these observations on the building's architecture in his book, *Robin Ward's Vancouver*:

> There are few buildings in Stanley Park. This is not the Tuileries or St. James's, surrounded by public architecture and criss-crossed by imperial vistas. Stanley Park's formal embellishments have been left to gardeners rather than emperors and architects.
>
> The attraction of the buildings in the park is their vernacular, rather than urban, quality. The Stanley Park Pavilion, the tea room built in 1911 in the Swiss chalet style popularized by the CPR, is a good example. It looks handmade from the trees that once stood in its garden. There's a picturesque, amateurish charm here — all gables and rustic disorder. This building is completely at home in its wooded setting.

The Stanley Park Pavilion was built in 1911 in the then-popular Swiss chalet style.
ROBIN WARD ILLUSTRATION. ROBIN WARD'S VANCOUVER, HARBOUR PUBLISHING 1990

Whether you're looking for fine dining or a light snack, the Pavilion is a fabulous deal. The cordon bleu cuisine prepared by students of the Dubrulle cooking school makes this restaurant a dining destination for people with little interest in exploring the rest of the park. The menu features main dishes such as Cedar Planked Salmon and Black Peppercorn Crusted Rack of Lamb for between $12 and $18. The Picnic Café offers more casual fare, including a wide assortment of salads, as well as smokies, burgers, and chicken on the grill for between $5 and $8. Or you can snack on a muffin and something hot for around $3. The engineer from the miniature railway was among the customers at the café on one of our visits.

The Vancouver Park Board band
assembled in front of the Pavilion, August 1925.
LEONARD FRANK PHOTO. VPL 11701

The patio is large and covered, with comfortable chairs and generous tables, and is surrounded by greenery. On a Saturday evening in August, only three of the dozen or more patio tables were occupied in the café area. The restaurant's smaller patio area was not much busier. And there are plenty of tables inside both the café and restaurant. The restaurant and café are wheelchair-accessible, as are the restrooms inside.

ROSE GARDEN AND SHAKESPEARE GARDEN

What's in a name?
That which we call a rose,
by any other name would smell as sweet.
WILLIAM SHAKESPEARE

We've had people from the Rose Society of Carolina come in saying how abominable our roses are," says the Park Board's Terri Clark. "We don't have a really great climate for roses." Roses thrive in a hot, dry Mediterranean climate. Our damp, mild weather promotes mildew and spectacular aphid infestations. But the roses in Stanley Park have one big plus — they've been off drugs for several years.

Since 1998, Stanley Park gardeners have been using an integrated pest-management plan in all the gardens. Leaves are used as mulch. Birds go through the leaves looking for plant-munching pests such as slugs. Weeds and morning glory are cleaned out by hand, rather than with herbicides. As a result, all of the gardens in the park are safe for people with environmental sensitivities. Rose snobs may not find the Rose Garden anything to write home about. But Clark says Stanley Park strives to find the right balance between esthetics and good environmental practice. "It's a generational thing, from the people who used

Agent Orange to people who don't want to use anything. We don't use chemicals unless it's crucial, and then we use the least amount of Safer's fungicide, then rope it off and put signs up. We don't do that to roses for a very good reason. We're trying to put in roses that don't require that, which is unfortunate because you don't get everything."

Those sniffy Carolina gardeners aside, rose fanciers will find hundreds of varieties to see and smell. Coastal BC has the warmest winter temperatures in Canada. We're zone eight hardy, which allows our gardeners to take risks the rest of Canada can only dream about. Folks from the prairies are pretty impressed by the display of thousands of roses in full bloom by late spring.

The gardens were originally laid out in the 1920s and 1930s. The Kiwanis Club oversaw the planting of the Rose Garden, while the Shakespeare Society hoped to replicate an Elizabethan garden across the road that would contain all the plants mentioned by the Bard. Now the two gardens are generally seen as one, and they're the crowning glory of the park's many plantings of perennial flowers and ornamental trees and shrubs, and the prime destination for gardeners, photographers, and wedding parties. If you're visiting in early summer, make sure to walk under the long arbour supporting the lavish display of old-fashioned roses and clematis. They're at their best at this time of year.

During the 1930s and 1940s the Park Board's original greenhouses were situated next to the Rose Garden to provide bedding plants for Vancouver parks. As the parks system expanded and more plants were needed, the greenhouses were moved, and are now next door to the Sunset Community Centre, on 51st Avenue just off Fraser Street. The Park Board still grows all its own annual flowers, about 350,000 plants each year, making it one of the leaders of civic horticulture in North America.

You'll have to look closely for the Shakespeare Memorial. It's tucked into an inconspicuous bed backed up against a fence along the north side of the garden, next to the service yard. Poor Shakespeare's profile appears to have been damaged and then patched up with cement. His nose looks like Bob Hope's.

A fixture in the Rose Garden that never fails to charm is the English-style bench near the road. The wood has been bleached silver-grey by the rain and sun. A brass plaque green with verdigris reads: "To A Gentle Lady", leaving visitors to speculate about the identity of the mysterious woman." The bench program continues to be a successful fundraiser for the Park Board. Donors can dedicate a bench that will be maintained for 10 years. The engravings on the plaques make for fascinating reading, and allow the visitor to conjure up life stories from the legends. The program has been so popular, there are now very few places left in Stanley Park where you can put up a bench.

The Rose and Shakespeare Gardens are easy to find. The bus into Stanley Park goes up Pipeline Road, which bisects the Rose Garden, and will drop you at the bus loop a short walk from the gardens. The Shakespeare Garden is just west of the Rose Garden. If you're driving, head west along Georgia Street. As you enter the Stanley Park Causeway, the extreme right-hand lane will bring you into the park. After you leave the causeway, there's a fork in the road. Bear right and you'll be diverted onto the Park Drive. Bear left and you'll find yourself on Pipeline Road, which parallels the right-of-way for Vancouver's water supply. Pipeline Road is a useful route if you want to lop off four kilometres from the Park Drive, and rejoin it as it makes its ascent to Prospect Point. Pipeline Road will take you directly to the Variety Kids' Farmyard, the miniature railway, Malkin Bowl, and the Pavilion. Further along, on the left, is Beaver Lake. Park your car on Pipeline Road (don't forget to pay for parking at one of the blue kiosks). The lake is a short stroll down Tisdall Walk.

WAR MEMORIALS

Before it was Stanley Park, the peninsula was held by the Dominion government of Canada, and considered a strategic military reserve. The young country's biggest worry was an attack by the United States. Third Beach was a good place to see, and defend against, the expected Yankee raiders. By 1888, relations between the United States and Canada had improved to the point where we no longer feared an invasion, and the federal government decided it was safe to accede to Vancouver's wish to use the land for a city park. It was a savvy decision to keep the parcel of land intact. Should the need ever arise again, it would be easier for the military to expropriate public parkland rather than private property.

Canadian-Japanese Memorial, 1920.
STUART THOMSON PHOTO. VA, CVA 99-3280

There are several reminders of war and military involvement throughout the park, from HMCS *Discovery* on Deadman's Island to the searchlights above Siwash Rock and the abandoned gun emplacements and ammunition magazine on Ferguson Point. Two of the more poignant war memorials can be found in the area around the Pavilion.

Behind the Pavilion, across the road from the bus loop, is the tiny Garden of Remembrance. It's all but hidden from view, with a stream trickling through the ferns and shrubs. There's a wishing well, and rocks are set into the ground inscribed with the names of air force squadrons from Czechoslovakia, Australia, England, New Zealand, and Vancouver. The air force women's auxiliary came up with the idea for the garden, designed by Park Board employees Alex Dixon and Bill Livingstone, in January 1948. The rocks came from around Vancouver, except for one small piece of carved stone taken from the Palace of Westminster (the Houses of Parliament) in London, England, which had been bombed during the Second World War.

In early spring the first trees to flower are the Japanese cherries. A path lined with these ravishing ornamentals leads to the Japanese War Memorial, just down the hill from the Pavilion, next to the Aquarium. It was erected in 1920 for Canadians of Japanese descent who had died fighting with the Canadian Expeditionary Force in the First World War. The base of the monument is lotus-shaped, with each petal of the lotus listing the names and dates of the battles in which the men fought. The loss of life was significant, especially at Ypres and Paschendaele. Rising from the centre of the base is a fluted obelisk topped by a lantern in the form of a pagoda. For several years the lantern was lit each night.

When the monument was built, relations between Japan and the British Empire were cordial. Those relations had changed drastically by 1941. The government of Canada impounded the property of Japanese-Canadians, seizing everything from homes to fishing boats. Men, women, and children were rounded up and incarcerated, first at a camp on the grounds of the Pacific National Exhibition on Hastings Street and later in internment camps far from the coast. Most of their property was never returned. During the Second World War, there were people who wanted the memorial bulldozed, but it endured, as have our Japanese-Canadian neighbours.

BELUGA AND BOY EXPERIENCE A CLOSE ENCOUNTER AT THE VANCOUVER AQUARIUM. CHRISTOPHER GRABOWSKI

RACCOONS ARE MIGHTY CUTE, BUT PLEASE DON'T FEED THEM.
IN FACT, THERE ARE HEAVY FINES FOR FEEDING THE WILDLIFE IN STANLEY PARK. KEVIN MILLER

In the late 1960s, people celebrated peace and love with Be-Ins at Brockton Point. On April 19, 1992, thousands flocked to the 25th anniversary Easter Be-In, where greying hippies and their kids and grandchildren listened to sixties' bands such as The Seeds of Time. Artist Bob Masse recreated one of his classic psychedelic posters for the occasion.

POSTER COURTESY OF BOB MASSE

"Coastal Defence Gun and Crew."
THIS PAINTING BY CAPTAIN EDWARD JOHN HUGHES REPRESENTS SECOND WORLD WAR GUN EMPLACEMENTS AT THIRD BEACH.

ACCESSION NUMBER 19710261-3870, BEAVERBROOK COLLECTION OF WAR ART, CANADIAN WAR MUSEUM

LIONS GATE BRIDGE AND SNOW-CAPPED NORTH SHORE MOUNTAINS SEEN FROM STANLEY PARK SEAWALL. STUART McCALL

"ALL ABOARD!" MINIATURE RAILWAY LIMITED EDITION ETCHING BY BARB WOOD

THE FOUNTAIN AT LOST LAGOON HAS BEEN A DAZZLING VANCOUVER LANDMARK FOR MORE THAN 60 YEARS. STUART McCALL

BENCHES THROUGHOUT THE PARK CARRY INSCRIPTIONS OF DEDICATION TO FRIENDS AND LOVED ONES. CHRISTOPHER GRABOWSKI

A WOLF'S TALE

At one time, Arctic wolves padded around in the enclosure through which the miniature railway runs. One Saturday night at the end of the summer, someone broke down part of the fence, and two white wolves escaped. Mike Mackintosh was assistant manager of the zoo at the time, and it fell to him and his boss Larry LeSage to round up the escapees.

"I was in a cold sweat," Mackintosh recalls. "I had a net, but I thought, what am I gonna do with a net with a wolf? Meanwhile, Larry and a police officer went roaring off after this one wolf over by the totem poles. They managed to get him cornered in one of the buildings, and Larry tranquillized him with a dart. And it isn't like after 30 seconds you fall over in a deep sleep. That's just a myth. It was more like a three-martini cocktail. So he sort of fell over, and he's still conscious, so Larry roars in there with a net and they manage to truss him up and put him in the back of the police car. They've got the flashing lights going, and they're backing up and this runner comes storming up, covered with sweat, and bug-eyed, and he says to the police officer, 'What's the matter with you guys? Why can't you look after the dogs in this park? I've been running on the Seawall and this big white dog's been nipping at my heels all the way along!'"

The other wolf led them on a merry chase through the park all night, stopping and waiting for its pursuers to catch up, then loping off again into the trees. Finally Mackintosh spotted him early next morning, waiting.

"It was really eerie," he remembers. "I came over the hill by the little stone bridge (at the west end of Lost Lagoon) and the field was shrouded in mist. And there, standing in the mist, was this wolf. We managed to get a tranquillizer into him and he was back in before eight o'clock and nobody knew the wolves had gone."

BABES IN THE WOODS

In a thousand acres of wilderness a stone's throw from a major urban area, you'd expect to find a few skeletons lurking, and Stanley Park has its share.

One of the most chilling crimes was discovered on a cold morning in January 1953. The skeletal remains of two children were found, covered by a woman's fur coat, and by leaves that had fallen from the trees since the children had died in the fall of 1947. The children's own clothes had rotted, as had most of their little leather Second World War flying helmets. A lunch box lay beside their bodies, along with a woman's shoe and an axe. The axe fit perfectly in the wound on the back of one of the skulls.

The other skull had been fractured, likely from a blow from the head of the same axe.

An artist recreated the children's faces from plaster casts of the skulls, and their clothing was replicated. Photographs of the recreations were distributed throughout North America, but to no avail. Rumours circulated that their distraught mother, who was unable to care for them, had killed the children. Speculation was that she then killed herself. None of the rumours could be substantiated, and the mystery deepened.

In 1998, DNA tests were done on the remains of the children, who were discovered to be brothers, not a boy and a girl as had previously been believed. A national television show, "Crime Stoppers," produced a segment on the case, which resulted in several more tips being received by police. But the case remains unsolved, open, and active. You can find out more about the case, and see the actual skulls, if you visit the Vancouver Police Museum in the old Coroner's Court on Cordova Street. (For information, call (604) 665-3346).

More recently, in November 2001, a man was savagely beaten to death with a baseball bat in what police say was a hate crime. It happened late at night, near a series of trails on the north side of Lost Lagoon used by gay men looking for casual sex. The practice is called "trail-hopping," and can be extremely dangerous.

In the spring of 2002, a young Korean exchange student was brutally beaten while jogging on a popular trail near Lost Lagoon. Alarmed residents were warned against running alone, and were advised to vary their routes and stay alert — good advice anywhere.

Despite these crimes, Stanley Park is remarkably safe for the eight million people who visit the park each year. By far the most common crime is the mundane but extremely annoying theft from automobiles. Thieves know that visitors to the park are often away from their cars for an hour or more. Visitors are reminded not to leave valuables in their cars, or at least to lock them away out of sight in the trunk. There is a police presence in the park, but they can't be everywhere at once.

VANCOUVER POLICE MOUNTED SQUAD

The Vancouver Police Department's Mounted Squad has overseen park security since 1909. The constables on horseback patrol the park's thousand acres and venture into the neighbouring West End and downtown core as needed. The squad is effective in major crowd control situations and makes a handsome escort when royalty comes to town.

There are currently seven two-legged members of the squad, and eight horses are stabled in the service yard near the Rose Gardens. The equine criteria for the job require a police horse to be a big, dark-coloured gelding of quiet disposition. The humans have to be First Class Constables with 80 hours of paddock training under their belts. The work seems pleasant and is largely geared towards public relations. Visiting tourists adore chatting up the officers (don't we all?) and kids are encouraged to approach each Mounted Squad member to request a trading card. Hey Kids! Collect all ten!

A member of the Vancouver Police Mounted Squad patrols the park. STUART McCALL

Bridges and stream in Ceperley Meadow, ca. 1920.   LEONARD FRANK PHOTO. VPL 8146

5 From Ceperley to Lost Lagoon

It is dusk on the Lost Lagoon
And we two dreaming the dusk away.
Pauline Johnson

VANCOUVER'S BACKYARD

Take any kid to Ceperley Park and they're bound to head straight to the big red fire truck. The dangerous bits have been removed or welded shut and countless layers of paint encase the chassis, so the only danger is supplied by kids' lively imaginations. And the biggest problem might be deciding who gets to drive.

That conflict can be resolved by taking them next door to the Stanley Park Traffic School. Back in the 1950s when the school started, the kids drove miniature Austin pedal cars supplied by a local dealership. A modern fleet of German-made Kettcars has since replaced the Austins. The only people more eager than the kids to take a turn at the wheel are the parents, who wish they were kids again. A Park Board playground leader and officers from the Vancouver Police Department run the traffic school. On weekday mornings children between the ages of five and eight learn the rules of the road, including how to recognize traffic lights, and how to signal and turn from the correct lanes. It's great fun and many a three-year-old is left wailing at curbside while an older sibling larks about in a little convertible. Group bookings can be arranged (*see page 118, bottom*) or you can sign your child up for a half-hour session on a first-come, first-served basis.

By dusk the Traffic School is packed away and the blacktop is filled with the whirling skirts of dancers. Usually, portable CD and tape players supply the music. But if you're in luck, on the nights reserved for Scottish dancing, members of the Vancouver Fiddle Orchestra will drop by to play tunes like "Culla Boy," "The Mayflower," and "Pelorus Jack," while up to 90 dancers whirl, and as many or more spectators watch from the sidelines. Some dancers wear kilts; others prefer skirts, shorts, or whatever they're comfortable in. Readers of Vancouver's weekly newspaper, the

Georgia Straight, voted the dusk dances as the "best kilts-optional event in Vancouver." On other nights, bystanders are invited to join in for some elementary folk dancing. When it's ballroom dancing night, the strains of a bossa nova or a tango drift over the playground as elegant couples perform the sexy and intricate dance steps.

Ceperley Park and Second Beach serve as Vancouver's backyard. On the neighbouring soccer pitch there's usually a vigorous game going on, while cyclists and rollerbladers whisk past. Mouth-watering aromas drift from the barbecue pits as families spread out their picnic suppers. Nearby, Second Beach offers logs to lean against and acres of sand sloping gently to the sea. Freighters ride at anchor as the sun slips below the sparkling waters of English Bay, and on soft summer nights it seems like there's no better place to be on earth.

STANLEY PARK TRAFFIC SCHOOL: Free
Beginning of July to the end of August
Monday to Friday, 10:00 a.m. to 1:30 p.m.
To arrange group bookings call the West End Community Centre
(604) 257-8333

DANCING IN THE PARK: Free
Mid-June to mid-August
Monday to Thursday, 7:30 p.m. to 9:30 p.m.

A SIEGE OF HERONS

The great blue heron has inhabited the earth for at least 60 million years, and perhaps twice that long. It's hard to get an exact read because birds' hollow bones don't make good fossils. But it's likely that ancestral herons were here long before the landform we know as Stanley Park existed. Watching them fly, you have to wonder how they ever survived.

Herons are stunningly awkward getting airborne, and sometimes it seems they'll never make it off the ground. Heaving their great wings, they slowly rise, dragging those long legs behind like the forgotten undercarriage of a 747. Once aloft, however, they are elegant gliders. Their two-metre wingspan allows them to cruise almost at stall speed. Like the takeoffs, the landings are also a little dicey, and you almost expect them to trip and plant their beaks into the sand.

According to the Canadian Wildlife Service, the great blue is the largest and most widely distributed kind of heron in Canada, ranging from Alaska to Mexico and the West Indies. Wisely, most herons head south during the cold Canadian winter, except in coastal BC, where the mild climate encourages them to stay all year.

A heron is a cunning fisher, employing stealth and patience along the rocky shoreline as it seeks its supper. The technique is simple. More than a metre tall on those stick-like legs, the heron

stands almost motionless in the shallow water, with only its head and eyes moving. Once it spots a small fish or shellfish, the heron stretches out its entire body, plunges its head into the water, catches the prey in its bill, then with a deft movement of its head drops the morsel headfirst into its gullet. Herons have also been seen diving underwater to catch fish. During the nesting season, they have that charming avian habit of regurgitating predigested food into the waiting mouths of their clamorous young. And what a racket those babies make.

The nests are unmistakable in the fall and winter, high up in the branches of deciduous trees. Like their inhabitants, the nests are large — a metre or more in diameter, with a central cavity or well, often lined with lichen or moss. In Stanley Park there are twelve to fifteen active nests scattered in four clumps among seven trees. In April, females lay up to five eggs, which take about a month to hatch. Males take care of incubation duties during the day, and the females take the night shift. Once the eggs are hatched, dad babysits during the day while mom hunts for food. At night, the roles are reversed.

Great blue heron.
KEVIN MILLER

Life isn't easy for heron chicks, and only the strong and the lucky survive. At two weeks of age they're already standing up in the nest, cleaning their plumage, stretching their wings, and competing for food. At six weeks, they're practicing for flight, jumping about in the nest and on branches, and beating their wings. By the time they're two months old, heron chicks are flying clumsily from tree to tree, then returning to their nest to be fed. This is a dangerous time for them. If a chick falls to the ground and is unable to return to the nest, the parents will not feed it. By ten weeks, heron chicks leave the nest and are independent. But not many survive to that stage.

Heron chicks are snack food for eagles, which maraud the nests mercilessly during the breeding season. When an eagle flies over a colony, every adult bird takes flight. The idea is to confuse the predator, and with all those clumsy birds flapping about, it sometimes works. But it also leaves the chicks undefended, or results in an adult heron being carried off by the eagle instead. You wouldn't expect a huge heron to be intimidated by the smaller bald eagle, but without flesh-eating beaks or talons, herons have no natural defence against these predators. Crows, which have no use for eagles, are an unlikely ally, and sometimes harass the predator. But crows are just as likely to snack on heron eggs and chicks. The Park Board's Mike Mackintosh recalls watching eagles attack a heron nest near the Aquarium.

"We'd be sitting there having coffee in the afternoon and someone would shout 'Incoming!'" he recalls. "The eagles would come in on these low-flying B-52 passes that would just send the herons into a panic. There'd be squawking and birds falling out of nests. It happens a lot, so there is a tremendous attrition."

The eagles may be simply the most spectacular of the predators. Raccoons, gulls, crows, and ravens also prey on both the eggs and the chicks. If the weather is cold and rainy in April, the chicks can freeze or drown in the nest. But loss of habitat, largely because of human development, is probably the biggest threat to the survival of urban herons. As a rule, there should be no development within 300 metres of a heron colony at all, and certainly no disturbance between March and August. So what's surprising is not that the number of nests is dwindling, but that there are as many herons as there are in Stanley Park.

In the 1920s there were more than three dozen heron nests near Brockton Point. By the mid-1970s, the heronry had relocated to a stand of trees near the Aquarium. The reason is unclear. Some naturalists think that herons move their nests when a predator takes an adult heron. One of the factors in locating near the Aquarium may have been the buckets full of fish being brought to the otters and other aquatic life. Whatever the reason, there were more than 40 nests in that heronry by the late 1970s. But their numbers have declined over the past quarter century, and in 2001, the heronry moved again. Now it's located near the tennis courts between the Rhododendron Garden and the Park Board office. Volunteers with the Stanley Park Ecology Society have counted 12 to 15 active nests in the area. The abundance of white guano on the pavement surrounding the nesting trees is a good indicator of their presence. You may also see greenish-blue eggshells, fish carcasses, and other detritus that has fallen from the nests. Once you see the signs, look up, look wa-a-a-ay up, and you'll likely spot their nests, even with the cover of leaves.

"People say, 'well, they wouldn't be here if there wasn't enough food,'" Mackintosh says.

"But the reason their colony is as tiny as it is, is there's really very little foreshore around Stanley Park. It's not like Boundary Bay where you've got lots of feed. You've got Second Beach and Third Beach, and then you've got sort of rocky shoreline along under the Narrows. But you don't have broad expanse of area that's subject to tidal action. So there isn't a great deal."

There is a heron colony established near the Canadian Forces Base in Chilliwack and another in Beacon Hill Park in Victoria. And while the population of the Stanley Park heronry fluctuates, it's still a viable colony.

Dalyce Epp is on the board of the Stanley Park Ecology Society, and is a member of the Canadian Society of Environ-mental Biologists. During the spring and summer of 2002, she kept a journal on the Stanley Park colony. By the end of May, she verified 7 deaths, both chicks and adults, because of eagle attacks. As of July, she had found 35 eggshells on the ground, and estimates that 13 of the chicks survived to adulthood.

Herons live up to 17 years, which gives them many chances to breed. And they have survived on the planet much longer than humans, despite predators, climate changes, and worse.

Like many of the quasi-natural situations in Stanley Park, the heron habitat may not be perfect, but it seems to be working.

A HOLE-IN-ONE

No time for a full round of golf? No worries. You can get in 18 holes in a couple of pleasant hours at the Stanley Park Pitch-and-Putt. The holes range from 40 to 100 yards. The fairways and greens are manicured and landscaped beautifully, with scarcely a sand trap or water hazard in sight. You can rent clubs (left- or right-handed) and buy balls at the clubhouse. All you need is a pitching wedge (or perhaps a seven-iron if you need more oomph) and a putter. Watch the oomph, though. Peter MacDougall, a Vancouver book representative, was golfing with a friend who shanked a long one.

*Stanley Park Pitch-and-Putt
golf course, 1940.*
DON COLTMAN, STEFFENS–COLMER PHOTO.
VA, CVA 586-31

The young men heard the inevitable crash and tinkle of broken glass and knew the ball had broken a car window. They steeled themselves to assess the damage and discovered the car they'd hit was their own. Our advice: play with finesse and don't park near the course. It's first-come, first-served, and you may have to wait a little while at each tee during the summer. But you can spend the time admiring the brilliant plumage of the Ted and Mary Greig Rhododendron Garden that surrounds the course.

The daily routine of several West End residents includes playing a round before breakfast. After one old duffer passed on, his son brought his ashes to the course and sprinkled a little bit of his dad in every cup.

STANLEY PARK PITCH-AND-PUTT (604) 681-8847
Open year round
Summer hours: 7:30 a.m. until dusk
Winter hours: 9:00 a.m. until dusk

TED AND MARY GREIG RHODODENDRON GARDEN

Alleyne Cook had to come halfway around the world to find his life's work. He arrived in Canada from New Zealand in the mid-1950s and his horticultural training and natural green thumb were a perfect match for Vancouver's gentle climate. He was particularly fond of rhododendrons, a family of more than 800 varieties of elegant flowering shrubs from Southern China and the Himalayas. Until Cookie arrived, rhododendrons were virtually unknown in Vancouver. He helped set up the Vancouver Rhododendron Society in 1955, and went to work for the Vancouver School Board. A decade later his expertise with rhodos caught the attention of the head of the Park Board.

"The phone rang one night and it was Bill Livingstone," Cookie recalls. "He said, 'We've bought all these rhododendrons from Vancouver Island, and nobody on the staff knows anything about them. Will you come work for us?'" There were 8,000 rhododendrons, all from the collection of Ted and Mary Greig, who were retiring from the nursery business on Vancouver Island. The collection was bought for $16,000, but was worth more than 10 times that amount, and is now considered to be priceless.

Cookie took the job on the understanding that they'd let him do what he felt was best with the rhodos. For the next 23 years,

Alleyne Cook began work on the Ted and Mary Greig Rhododendron Garden in the 1960s. The garden now contains more than 3,000 plants. BARBARA COOK

that's exactly what he did. He began by creating 10 beds near the tennis courts, close to the densely populated neighbourhood of the West End, between Stanley Park and downtown Vancouver.

"The ultimate aim was to have enough colour, enough beds here, to bring the people out of those apartments. This bed here," says Cookie, pointing with his blackthorn cane to the bed between the tennis courts and the West End, "was pure clay, and we estimated we put 10 feet of leaves on it, and turned the clay into the most beautiful loam you could ever find. It kept down the weeds. So simply through birds and animals and healthy growth, we had no need for herbicides or pesticides or anything. This is a healthy garden for people with asthma or allergies or anything like that."

Now the Ted and Mary Greig Rhododendron Garden contains more than 3,000 rhodos, and encircles the park's pitch-and-putt golf course. With the crook of his cane, Cookie hooks a branch toward him to inspect the blossoms. Some of the towering rhododendrons are 50 years old. Many come from Cookie's own garden.

"That's one of my wedding presents," he says, pointing past the tenth tee on the pitch-and-putt. "Barbara and I have been married 40 years, so you know exactly how much that grows in 40 years. Because you have space in a park, you can just leave things to grow. It's like a laboratory, and it's very nice to know how big a plant will grow in a benign climate if it's not pruned and cut back."

Benign indeed. Vancouver's moist and temperate climate is almost ideal for rhododendrons, and their cousins, azaleas. So Cookie used the Greig garden as a nursery for some of the west coast's best public gardens. In the late 1970s, 3,000 of the prized rhodos were moved from Stanley Park to the Sino-Himalayan Garden at Van Dusen Botanical Gardens (37th and Granville) in Vancouver. Others have gone to gardens in the United States and Canada. And while many of these gardens charge admission, the glorious Greig garden is free for everyone to enjoy.

The Camellia Walk, along the south side of the golf course, was, with a few exceptions, created from camellias from the West End. Many of the old houses and smaller apartment buildings in that area of the city were being torn down in the 1960s and 1970s, to be replaced by high-rise apartments. The camellias in the gardens would have been taken to the dump. So Cookie and his crew rescued them.

The Greig Garden circumnavigates the pitch-and-putt golf course and is a pleasant, 90-minute stroll. The best time for blooms is between late April and early July, with May and June the prime months.

TEA AT THE FISH HOUSE

The Arts and Crafts-style building tucked in behind the tennis courts and the golf course was designed as a pavilion to serve the sportsmen and women of years gone by. Currently a private restaurant, The Fish House, operates on the top two floors. The ground level still serves as a clubhouse, with public change rooms and a concession.

The Fish House is a standout in a city filled with delectable restaurants. Since the mid-1990s, the kitchen has been run by chef Karen Barnaby, a cook devoted to serving fresh, local ingredients, simply but perfectly prepared. The container garden on the second-floor balcony is not just window dressing. The flowers and herbs regularly show up in the meals prepared in the kitchen below. The Fish House serves the tastiest Caesar salad in the city, according to the annual Best of Vancouver poll in the city's weekly newspaper, the *Georgia Straight*.

The Fish House is pricey, but there's an economical way to experience the benefits of kitchen and décor — afternoon tea. One of the finer customs adopted by the colonials, the full cream tea is served from 2:00 to 4:00 p.m., seven days a week.

The selection of savouries is formidable — cured salmon on graham bread, cucumber and goat cheese fingers, organic currant scones, and asiago biscuits. The tray of sweets is divine — mini crèmes brûlées, chai-spiced butter balls, and lemon curd tarts. And of course there are the never-empty pots of tea. Sherry and champagne are available for those who have something to celebrate. All this, plus a view of the exquisitely tended gardens, for only $20 per person. Tea at the Fish House will subdue the most difficult guest and you probably won't need to follow it with supper.

Sad but true, the Ferguson Point Teahouse does not serve an afternoon tea. You can grab a nice cup of tea and a treat at the Pavilion's Gourmet Picnic café all year round, and its dining

The Fish House Restaurant.
PHOTO COURTESY THE FISH HOUSE

room has been used for the occasional tea dance. But so far, the only place in Stanley Park to indulge in the charming ritual of afternoon tea is the Fish House.

FISH HOUSE RESTAURANT (604) 681-7275
Handicapped parking and wheelchair accessible.
Parking off Lagoon Drive.

LOST LAGOON AND WATERFOWL

Once upon a time you could rent rowboats on Lost Lagoon and scull serenely among the swans and ducklings, or even go under the pretty stone bridge where the willows weep and the water drains slowly away into Ceperley Meadow. The older kids told the younger ones that Lost Lagoon was a bottomless hole where dead bodies were dumped. It was a place of romance and mystery. In 1929, the 42-acre lake was stocked with cutthroat trout, and you could rent a rod and reel and try your luck. Now only a few lazy carp patrol the bottom of the lagoon. And once in a generation, there's a cold snap that freezes the water until it's thick enough to skate on.

Lost Lagoon was originally a saltwater tidal basin between Coal Harbour and English Bay. At times the basin would be in flood, and it was possible to canoe from one body of water to the other. When the tide was low, the area was reduced to mud flats, a good source of clams for the local residents. Mohawk poet Pauline Johnson lived in the West End, and Stanley Park was her backyard. She often paddled her canoe on the waters of Coal Harbour. But she never did like the name.

"I have always resented that jarring, unattractive name," she wrote. "When I first ... idled about the margin, I named the sheltered little cove the Lost Lagoon. This was just to please my own fancy, for as that perfect summer month drifted on, the ever-restless tides left the harbour devoid of water at my favourite canoeing hour, and my pet idling place was lost for many days; hence my fancy to call it Lost Lagoon." Her poem recalls a more sylvan time.

O! Lure of the Lost Lagoon

It is dusk on the Lost Lagoon,
And we two dreaming the dusk away,
Beneath the drift of a twilight grey,
Beneath the drowse of an ending day,
And the curve of a golden moon.

It is dusk on the Lost Lagoon,
And gone are the depths of haunting blue,
The grouping gulls, and the old canoe,
The singing Firs, and the dusk and — you,
And gone is the golden moon.

O! lure of the Lost Lagoon, —
I dream tonight that my paddle blurs
The purple shade where the seaweed stirs,
I hear the call of the singing firs
In the hush of the golden moon.

Once in a generation, there's a cold snap that freezes the water in Lost Lagoon until it's thick enough to skate on.
STUART THOMSON PHOTO. 1929, VA, CVA 99-1976

Pauline Johnson died in Vancouver on March 7, 1913. A cairn at Ferguson Point near Third Beach marks her grave. Following the dedication of this monument in 1922, the Park Board officially named Lost Lagoon in her honour.

By the early 1920s, a causeway had been built that permanently cut off the tidal flats from Coal Harbour, creating a small, deep, freshwater lake in the tidal basin. Lost Lagoon soon became an ideal refuge for waterfowl.

Stanley Park is now home to a resident flock of between 200 and 300 Canada geese and about a dozen mute swans, and most of them nest around Lost Lagoon. Some of the swans come from golf courses and from other municipalities. Quite a few of them were captured by the Canadian Wildlife Service, which had been removing mute swans from the Fraser River delta south of Vancouver. The feral mute swans were disrupting the breeding of the native swans, prompting concerns about interbreeding. Several mute swans were going to be destroyed, so Mike Mackintosh of the Vancouver Park Board asked if he could relocate some of them to Stanley Park. The only condition was that the swans be pinioned. The pinion is the terminal segment of a bird's wing, and by slicing the tendon, the bird is rendered flightless.

"It's painless, and done under general anaesthetic," Mackintosh explains. "All of our mute swans have to be pinioned because they are not native birds, and according to provisions of our permit, they're not allowed to fly away (or) interbreed with other species."

Canada geese are another story. In the early 1960s, the Canada goose population was declining, particularly in western North America. Wildlife groups began to reclaim wetlands and to introduce breeding pairs. The Canada geese in Stanley Park responded beautifully, showing an ingenious knack for survival. They nested on the ground at first, but under the threat of heavy foot traffic, the geese started moving their nests to stumps left over from the early logging days. As the goose population grew and more people came to the park, the geese moved their nests to higher stumps.

"Some of them were on top of these huge cedar spars in the golf course, probably 50 feet up," recalls Mike Mackintosh. "The young, much like wood ducks, would be like India rubber balls. Their bones aren't really formed and they'd slip down the side of the tree and trundle off after mom to the water." Within a decade, though, the Canada goose repopulation program in Stanley Park had proven too successful.

"In the early seventies, I can vividly recall the sky being almost black over Lost Lagoon as they flew in," Mackintosh said. "There were more than 3,000 birds there sometimes. They spread out from Stanley Park into the West End, taking up residence on any balcony or rooftop they could find. They can eat up to a pound of grass a day, often pulling it up by the roots. Most of it comes out the other end of the goose."

With the rapid development of Vancouver's waterfront there was less green space for the geese, so most of them gathered in Stanley Park. Concerns that avian cholera and other diseases could wipe out not only the geese, but other birds as well, had people clamouring for control.

The same story was playing out in urban centres across Canada and the United States, and much effort was spent trying to get rid of the geese. Scaring them away with dogs didn't work because the dogs tended to herd the birds into swimming pools and backyards. Other municipalities relocated the geese, but the relocation camps soon filled up. Some people suggested slaughtering the geese and serving them up to the hungry and homeless. In the 1980s, the Vancouver Park Board decided instead on birth control. Yet even that solution raised problems.

Vasectomies are expensive — about $140 per gander. Taking the eggs away doesn't work,

"Gander the Gallant." A Canada goose protects its nest on the tree stump from Mounted Squad constable Cliff Cooper and horse Trouper.

RAY MUNRO PHOTO, MAY 1954, *The Vancouver Province*

because the geese will just lay more. Coating them with mineral oil prevents the eggs from hatching, but you have to oil them before the chicks develop inside the egg, otherwise the goose will keep sitting on them forever, eventually starving to death. The simplest solution is to addle, or shake the eggs. A few eggs will hatch, and the juveniles are removed to other wetlands where goose populations are lower. If they're removed early enough, the youngsters will imprint on the new habitat, and return there every year.

"I happen to like geese," Mike Mackintosh declares. "The problem is maintaining a healthy balance with the environment that is afforded them. Where there were vast sprawling areas of undeveloped land before, there is nothing left. And these birds are still here. They don't just disappear overnight."

The birth control approach seems to have worked because the population has stabilized. In the 1970s, Park Board crews routinely rounded up more than 2,000 geese and trucked them out to other habitats in the Fraser Valley. In 2002, for the first time in 30 years, that wasn't necessary. So the grassy shores of Lost Lagoon are once again easily explored without too much slipping and sliding on what the geese leave behind. There are several viewing platforms around Lost Lagoon and Beaver Lake for visitors to enjoy the waterfowl and other wildlife without disturbing nesting areas.

It's mandatory to keep dogs on a leash around geese and swans — as much for the dogs' safety as for the birds'. An irate gander protecting a nest has been known to take on a police officer mounted on a horse. Lesser creatures may not fare as well. And leave that bag of bread crumbs at home. It's illegal to feed the wildlife in the park, and there are hefty fines imposed. Besides, bread crumbs and popcorn make a poor diet for the birds.

The low-slung building on the eastern shore of Lost Lagoon is the Nature House, where the Stanley Park Ecology Society runs educational programs. Birders record their sightings in a logbook kept at the Nature House, and visitors from all over the world stop in and sign the guest book. The Society runs urban camping programs for kids in grades five to seven in the spring and fall. During the summer, a small army of volunteer Eco-Rangers patrols the park. They provide lots of useful information for visitors interested in the park's natural history. The Society also offers walking tours of the park for a small fee — check the calendar of events on the Web site listed opposite.

The fountain that graces the centre of Lost Lagoon was built for just $35,000 in 1936 to mark Vancouver's fiftieth birthday. If the Lions Gate Bridge could be compared to a strand of pearls, then the fountain was surely the park's tiara. To wartime Vancouver, it was the city's most glamorous spectacle, dazzling car passengers and drawing admirers out for an evening stroll. The spray, illuminated by coloured lights, was like a constant burst of fireworks reflected back in the murky mirror of the lagoon. Generations of kids would hold their breath as they rounded the curve off the bridge, waiting for their first glimpse of the fountain.

A group of UBC engineers, up to their annual hijinks, planted a VW Beetle on top of the fountain's jets in the early 1970s. The fountain was upgraded in 1986 as part of Vancouver's centennial celebration. It's no longer the showstopper it once was — our annual fireworks competition has conditioned us to expect sky-wide, high-voltage displays — but when the lights are lit and the jets throw up a glittering, rainbow-coloured spray, there's still a hint of the old-time magic at play.

The fountain at Lost Lagoon
lights up the evening.
W. J. MOORE PHOTO, 1936. VA, ST PK N142.05

STANLEY PARK ECOLOGY SOCIETY:

www.stanleyparkecology.ca

BRENDA HEMSING

6 Beaver Lake and Other Trails

We want to leave nature to handle her own affairs.

Mike Mackintosh, Vancouver Park Board

RAVINE TRAIL TO BEAVER LAKE

PERHAPS THE PRETTIEST FOREST TRAIL IN ALL OF Stanley Park is the ten-minute walk connecting the Seawall to Beaver Lake, following Beaver Lake Creek. The stone bridge just past Lumberman's Arch starts cars on their ascent to Prospect Point. Step under the bridge's arch, and leave the Seawall behind as you enter an emerald cavern furnished with trees, moss, a tumbling stream, and rustic wooden bridges. The light is filtered through branches far overhead, and trickling water is the foreground sound. Birds dart from branch to branch, and if you visit during the spring or fall you'll hear some of the migratory songbirds. You'll certainly see a slug or two oozing along the path. These slow-moving sacs of slime easily impress out-of-town visitors. For the record, slugs are snails without the shell. They're the sanitation engineers of the park, cleaning up everything in their path.

The eastern grey squirrel is a bold little character found all over the park, but its tinier cousin, the Douglas squirrel, is more elusive. Eight breeding pairs of eastern grey squirrels were introduced into Stanley Park around 1914 — a gift from Central Park in New York. Like a gang of brash, Bronx hoodlums, they took over the joint, ousting the Douglas squirrels to become Stanley Park's predominant rodent. Over the decades, grey squirrels have moved into surrounding neighbourhoods and are now found living miles away in Burnaby and New Westminster. Slowly, but inexorably, the grey squirrel diaspora appears to be heading back east.

Though harder to find, there are still good numbers of Douglas squirrels in Stanley Park. These reddish-brown squirrels have huge eyes and chatter a mile a minute. You may come across one of their middens, a pile of mostly cone scales from a

Douglas fir — their favourite treat. There are also flying squirrels in the park, and although they're considered a common animal, they're rarely seen. And if you take the Ravine Trail at dusk, you'll certainly hear the toads and tree frogs, and perhaps see a few bats as you approach Beaver Lake.

BEAVER LAKE

There are no beaver in Beaver Lake. There aren't any moose either, although you almost expect to see one in the morning mist, legs planted knee-deep in the water, raising its big head to gaze balefully at visitors while it continues to munch on a mouthful of dripping vegetation. That carpet of Chinese water lilies all but covering the surface of the lake was introduced around 1936, for the park's jubilee. The same plants were tried in Lost Lagoon with little success. But in Beaver Lake, they took with a vengeance. They're lovely in the early summer, nearly blanketing the entire surface with lotus-like blossoms. Unfortunately the lilies are starving the lake of oxygen, advancing its metamorphosis to marshland.

Grey squirrels are not native to Stanley Park. Eight breeding pairs were introduced into the park in 1914 as a gift from Central Park in New York.
CHRISTOPHER GRABOWSKI

Human interference has a lot to do with the way Beaver Lake has evolved. Years ago the Vancouver Angling Society envisioned a fish hatchery and stocked the lake with steelhead and other varieties of trout. A few trout and carp still exist, gasping after the precious bubbles of oxygen remaining in the lake, but fishing hasn't been allowed for decades. Painted turtles sun themselves on rocks along the shore, the offspring of abandoned pets, no doubt. There are also bullfrogs, released by an entrepreneur who tried and failed to capture the local frog-legs market. Neither the turtles nor the frogs are native to the lake.

Along with these interlopers, there's an abundance of indigenous wildlife in and around Beaver Lake. Ducks and geese paddle about in the murky water, leading their young to safety at the approach of humans. Great blue herons stand still as statues, looking for their supper. Woodpeckers, flycatchers, warblers, tanagers, and grosbeaks fill the surrounding forest with their song in the spring and summer. In the evening, bats flit over the water, gobbling their weight in moths, lacewings, and mosquitoes. And through the woods, shrews, squirrels, coyotes, skunks, and other small mammals hunt and are hunted.

The wildlife is just a fraction of what used to thrive around what the Salish people called Ahka-Chu, or little lake. Blacktail deer, elk, cougar, and black bear were common 150 years ago. But as the surrounding forest was opened up by human activities such as logging and recreation, the larger mammals sought wilder country.

The little lake is shrinking, and will one day disappear. In 1938 it measured 16.5 acres. By 1985, it had shrunk to just 10.5 acres. In most places it's scarcely a metre deep. Inexorably, the lake will become a swamp and the swamp a meadow. If we let it be long enough, the meadow will eventually become a forest. While human hands have hastened the evolution, it's a natural enough process. And there is much to explore as it happens.

BATS

Park your primordial fears at the door for a moment, and consider the amazing feat of engineering that is a bat. Flitting through the dark at speeds up to 180 k.p.h., a bat can snick an insect out of the air quicker than it takes to tell, sometimes using its tail to flip the tasty morsel up to its mouth. It can also hover like a helicopter if need be. A bat is a virtuoso in flight, so there's little chance it will get tangled up in your hair, even if you have a two-foot-tall 'do like Marge Simpson. If a bat can find a moth in the middle of the air over Beaver Lake after dark, it shouldn't have too much trouble avoiding you.

Now let's put another fear to rest. Yes, there are vampire bats. But they live in Central and South America. And they feed on large livestock, puncturing two neat pinholes near the neck, then taking just a teaspoon or two of blood. To cows or horses, it's not much more than a horsefly might take. And no, the livestock don't turn into the living dead.

The half dozen species of bats in Stanley Park don't drink warm blood. They're after insects. The Townsend's big-eared bat (also known as the western big-eared bat or the lump-nosed bat) treats Beaver Lake like a buffet. It dines on dung beetles, sawflies, lacewings, mosquitoes, and moths. Townsend's is on the smaller end of the scale for BC bats. It weighs just over eight grams, about the same as a loonie coin, with a wingspan of about 30 centimetres. The bats hang out in the deep forest during the day, sometimes nestling into the folds of the bark on hemlock or Douglas fir trees. In the evening they come out to eat their weight in bugs.

Like many bats in the northern hemisphere, Townsend's mates in the fall and early winter. But through a process called delayed fertilization, the eggs don't start growing until the spring, ensuring the females have recovered from the debilitating effects of hibernation. The pups are born in early summer, weighing just a couple of grams. Female bats usually have only one pup at a time, but most of the youngsters survive.

Unlike most other bats in BC, the Townsend's doesn't fly south in the fall. Instead, it gathers in colonies in mine shafts and caves or in old tree stumps in Stanley Park. Its heart rate drops from 100 beats a minute to 5, and it sleeps the winter away. It seems like a pretty good life. But the Townsend's big-eared bat is running out of habitat in southern BC. It likes to live at low altitudes, exactly the same places favoured by humans. Guess who's winning.

Still, you can see them flitting around after dark over Lost Lagoon or Beaver Lake, not much bigger than the dragonflies that hover near the water during the day. Stand very still, and with the dark bowl of the sky showing stars on a clear night, thrill to the whirring of the leatherwinged bats over the water.

THE STANLEY PARK ECOLOGY SOCIETY offers bat tours suitable for kids and adults. The cost is minimal, and the experience memorable. Call 604-257-8544. Or check out the Web site: www.stanleyparkecology.ca

SIWASH ROCK TRAIL

The Siwash Rock Trail follows the coastline along the sandstone bluffs 18 metres above the Seawall. These Burrard Formation walls are striped with coal and thin ribs of sedimentary rock tough enough to resist erosion by wind, waves, and rain. The grade is steep but the views will reward your effort. This hour-long walk packs in the best Stanley Park has to offer. There are ancient trees, staggering views of English Bay, and the remnants of military fortifications from both World Wars.

Pick up the trail just past Prospect Point (if you set off from Third Beach it's an uphill slog). Keep bearing right; the rule is to choose the paths that get you closest to the edge overlooking the Seawall. Not far in from the Park Drive is a mossy set of stairs leading down to a lower trail. The decaying sign is sprouting mushrooms, but the words Merilees Trail can still be seen. If you bear right, you'll soon be on the Siwash Rock Trail. A sturdy log fence keeps walkers on the path. Don't climb over it — the only shortcut down to the Seawall is a sheer drop.

You're in the heart of the old forest on these trails, and there's a touch of menace in the strange shapes of uprooted and prone trees. The girth of some of these fallen giants is awe-inspiring. A child could stand upright in the hollow cavity of a downed cedar. You wonder what could bring down such a massive and ancient entity. Even more remarkable is the powerful fecundity in this green world. On the trunk of a Douglas fir, ferns grow thick and lush as a chenille bedspread. From the stump of a long-gone cedar, a mature western hemlock grows straight, nursing off the acidic remains of the dead wood. The hemlock's days are already numbered — the parasitic dwarf mistletoe insinuates itself around the trunk, and will eventually topple the tree.

Soon you're near the cliff's edge and your first glimpse of Siwash Rock and the Seawall. Siwash Rock was formed about 35 million years ago when volcanic pressure split the sedimentary rock away from the main formation. The black magma cooled quickly, forming a basaltic skin that's tough enough to withstand the relentless efforts of sea, wind, and UBC engineering students.

The gravel trail is part of the perimeter road that originally circled the park. It leads to a lookout jutting over the Seawall directly behind Siwash Rock. This is the payoff for all your exertions — a bird's-eye view of Siwash Rock and a fresh perspective on the undulations of the Seawall. And you're standing on a piece of Vancouver's military history.

The lozenge-shaped structure was installed by the Royal Canadian Artillery during the First World War as a mount for a heavy-gauge gun. During the Second World War the bunker became a platform for a big searchlight, in anticipation of Japanese submarines that never came.

Stanley Park benches provide a peaceful spot to relax and soak up the view. ROB CARLSON

A DEDICATED VIEW

The Tower Court Morning Boys have been meeting at 5:30 every Monday, Wednesday, and Friday morning for close to two decades to run the nine kilometres around the seawall. Their name comes from the racquet club they belong to, although these days there are a number of women among the dozen or so runners. In the winter when it's dark and slippery, they use the Park Drive. George McLachrie has to leave his home in the Vancouver suburb of Coquitlam at 5 a.m. "It takes discipline," he says, "especially when it's dark and raining in the winter."

His running mates honoured George's dedication with a bench that commands a panoramic view of downtown Vancouver across Coal Harbour from the Seawall. The inscription on the plaque reads: "To George McLachrie in celebration of his 50th birthday from Tower Court's Morning Boys, November 25, 1990."

There are hundreds of these benches in Stanley Park (and in public parks around Vancouver), and each one tells a story. They're donated by people who want to remember a loved one. For around $1,800, donors get a bench and a small plaque bearing an inscription of their choice. The donation includes maintenance of the bench for 10 years.

"We've found this is the kind of way people like to give money to the park," explains the Park Board's Terri Clark. "Ordinary folk can afford something like this and it also gives us a bench. So it's a good trade-off. After 10 years we don't take their plaque off, but if it starts to fall apart, we'll ask if they want to rededicate the bench, or we can offer to put in a new one for somebody else."

Another of our favourite benches is in the Rose Garden, dedicated "To a Gentle Lady." It's a delicious mystery, leaving us to wonder if the lady was mistress, a mother, a wife, a daughter, or a friend? Most of the benches invite similar musings about the stories behind the dedications.

Stanley Park is running out of spots to put benches. But there is no shortage of people who wish to honour their friends and relatives, dead or alive, with a dedicated bench. Take advantage of the view they offer, and think for a moment about the people whose gift it is, and the person being honoured. And, as it says on Bill and Jacqui's bench at Ferguson Point, "Please Enjoy."

ACKNOWLEDGEMENTS

The Stanley Park Ecology Society helped us rediscover this wonderful park through their educational materials and programs. Brian Bedford, SPES manager of public programs, shared his enthusiasm along with his time and expertise. The Society uses a term that catches our fancy with its plain-spoken integrity. When ascertaining the accuracy of a set of directions, one of the Society's members will "ground-truth" them. That is, they will walk through the woods to see if the written directions bear an exact semblance to the truth.

While researching this book we attempted to ground-truth everything we wrote about. We ate the fish and chips, walked and cycled the Seawall and trails in fair weather and foul, and we gathered people's stories about the park and its pleasures. Our son, Nick, practiced his own form of ground-truthing, taking girlfriends to Prospect Point and the Brockton Point lighthouse to check out the view.

Terri Clark and Mike Mackintosh of the Vancouver Park Board provided a great deal of background to the park's story, and their personal understanding of it. Their candour and excellent memories are greatly appreciated. Eric Meagher's extensive forestry expertise helped us explain the effect of heavy weather on the trees in Stanley Park. Alleyne and Barbara Cook shared their genteel passion for rhododendrons, their time and their personal photographs. Likewise, Evelyn and Lorne Atkinson and Anne Duke entrusted us with irreplaceable family photos. As the honorary historian of the Royal Vancouver Yacht Club, Jock Ferrie was generous not only with his time and memories, but also with the club's treasured annals. And George McLachrie was gracious in sharing the story behind his bench overlooking Coal Harbour.

Our dear friends Eileen Mosca, Sarah Groves, Irene Robinson, Evelyn Harris and Joan Meister were more than generous with their time, their knowledge, their reference materials and their memories. And in the beginning there was Julian Ross. *The Stanley Park Companion* started with him, and we're grateful that he entrusted us with its telling.

For historical detail we've been greatly helped by the City of Vancouver Archives and by the Vancouver Public Library Special Collections. And some of our best sources have been local authors.

Blood, Donald A., *Townsend's Big-eared Bat*. Wildlife Branch, BC Ministry of Environment, Lands, and Parks, 1998.

Carver, John Arthur, *The Vancouver Rowing Club*. Aubrey F. Roberts Ltd., 1980.

Cran, George A., ed., *Annals of the Royal Vancouver Yacht Club (1903-1965)*. Evergreen Press.

D'Acres, Lilia and Donald Luxton, *Lions Gate*. Talonbooks, 1999.

Kluckner, Michael, *Vancouver: The Way it Was*. Whitecap Books, 1984.

MacCrostie, M. Watson, ed., *Annals of the Royal Vancouver Yacht Club (1971-1985)*. D.W. Friesen, Ltd.

Morley, Alan, *From Milltown to Metropolis*. Mitchell Press, 1974.

Naming, Opening and Dedication of Stanley Park 1888-1889, City Archives, City Hall, Vancouver, 1959.

Perry, Lisa, et al., *Beaver Lake Ecological Studies, vol. 2*. Environmental Science Program, Capilano College, 1998.

Steele, Richard, *The Stanley Park Explorer*. Whitecap Books, 1985.

Vancouver Natural History Society, *The Natural History of Stanley Park*. Discovery Press, 1988.

Ward, Robin, *Robin Ward's Vancouver*. Harbour Publishing, 1990.

SUGGESTED READING

Barnaby, Karen, *The Pacific Passions Cookbook: Celebrating the Flavours of the West Coast*. Whitecap Books, 1995.

Gold, Glen David, *Carter Beats the Devil*. Hyperion, 2002.

Gray, Charlotte, *Flint and Feather: The Life and Times of E. Pauline Johnson, Tekahionwake*. Harper Collins, 2002.

Parish, Roberta, and Sandra Thomson, *Tree Book: Learning to Recognize Trees of British Columbia*, 2nd ed. Forest Service Information Division, Province of British Columbia/ Forestry Canada, n.d.

Taylor, Timothy, *Stanley Park*. Knopf Canada, 2001.

Wilson, Ethel, *Swamp Angel*. Macmillan, 1954.

Index

Ron Bell
Suite 6
7148 Ash Crescent
Vancouver, BC.
V6P 3K7
June 20, 2003